ELVIS
75TH BIRTHDAY
UNSEEN ARCHIVES

ELVIS

75TH BIRTHDAY

UNSEEN ARCHIVES

Marie Clayton

PaRragon

Bath · New York · Singapore · Hong Kong · Cologne · Delhi · Melbourne

This edition published by Parragon in 2009

Parragon
Queen Street House
4 Queen Street
Bath, BA1 1HE, UK

Text © Parragon Books Ltd
For details of photographs, see pages 382–383

Produced by Atlantic Publishing
Design and origination by Cambridge Publishing Management Ltd

ISBN 978-1-4075-8096-8

Printed in China

Contents

Introduction

Elvis Presley burst onto the American music scene in 1956, although he had been well-known locally around Memphis for some time beforehand. He quickly became synonymous with the new rock 'n' roll music and teenagers everywhere took him to their hearts. His sensual performing style whipped his female fans into a frenzy, which initially caused much criticism in the press – but the resulting publicity did his career no harm at all. After he was drafted and did his service in the US army, without complaint or favors, opinion about him in the press began to change, and on his return his new, mature style helped him to reach an even wider audience.

Not content with being perhaps the world's most popular singer, he also moved into acting and soon took Hollywood by storm. During his career he made 31 movies – all of which were a success at the box office – and in the middle of the 1960s he was the highest-paid actor in Hollywood. After he returned to the concert stage in the 1970s his shows in Las Vegas were legendary, and he was soon dubbed the 'World's Greatest Entertainer'.

Elvis Presley: Unseen Archives charts the fascinating life of Elvis, right from his humble beginnings to his tragic death as a superstar and its aftermath. The exciting collection of photographs featured not only show him performing, but also include candid shots documenting his private life and a comprehensive selection of stills taken during the making of his movies. Many of the photographs are not clearly dated in the archives, but in this book they have been carefully placed in context with what was happening in his career at around the time they were taken. The pictures are accompanied by detailed and perceptive captions, which give a rounded portrait of the world's most famous singer. Elvis Presley was a phenomenon and his legacy continues to captivate people even today – the King may be dead, but his memory lingers on.

Elvis Presley
Unseen Archives

Chapter One

Love Me Tender

When Elvis Presley was born on 8 January 1935, few people could have predicted that he would go on to live the 'American dream'. His family were so poor they could not afford proper medical care; as a result his older twin brother, Jesse, was stillborn – a loss that was never to be forgotten, either by his mother, Gladys, or by Elvis himself. In the following years the family moved around Mississippi. Vernon, Elvis's father, had a series of jobs and Gladys too often had to work to support the family; and, when things got too tough, they simply moved on. Elvis was very close to his mother – particularly after his father was imprisoned for several months for forging a cheque – and she was very protective of her only surviving child.

Elvis grew up in a series of homes close to black neighbourhoods and, as a result, enjoyed black R&B, jazz and soul music from his earliest years, never regarding it as something separate from his own life as most white people did at the time. His family was closely involved with the church – particularly Gladys, who often attended several times a day – and Elvis was brought up to the sounds of gospel music, joining in as soon as he was able. Gladys also listened to country and western music on the radio at home, and Elvis was quick to learn all the songs.

Despite their circumstances, Gladys insisted that Elvis learn good manners and show respect to his elders – a grounding that stayed with him for the rest of his life. She constantly impressed upon him that he was special and different from other people. He grew up rather shy and dreamy, something of a loner, and music became a release from the constraints of his life. His family had no money to pay for lessons so he taught himself to play the piano and learnt guitar from family friends. With a good memory for words and music, he was able to sing or play a song after hearing it just once or twice. He entered his first singing competition at the age of 10, coming second and winning $5 plus free admission to some fairground rides.

Moving to Memphis in 1948, the Presleys lived near Beale Street, the legendary home of the blues. Moving his body while he was singing was something Elvis had already learnt from gospel singers but, in Memphis, he also learnt from the way the black singers he saw there moved. He came to admire their sense of style and colour, and in his teens began to develop his own look, which combined bold colours and sharp tailoring with long, slicked-back hair and sideburns. Typical outfits included a bolero jacket bought from Lanskys – a tailor on Beale Street – and trousers with a bright stripe down the side of the leg, and a bright-pink suit teamed with white suede shoes. It was very different from the cropped, preppy look of most other teenagers of the time. At first, Elvis aspired to be a gospel singer, but he also played hillbilly music and soon developed his own sound – a sound that was unlike that of any of the well-known singers of the time, but that later became known as rockabilly and then rock 'n' roll.

Sam Phillips and Marion Keisker had opened a recording studio in Memphis, mainly to record the music played by black artists. Sometime during the summer of 1953, Elvis – by that time working as a truck driver – turned up on their doorstep to record something and to let Sam hear him sing. Nothing happened for some time, but eventually Sam called him back and teamed him with two more experienced musicians: guitarist Scotty Moore and bass player Bill Black. After much rehearsing and several false starts as they found their way together, the three of them recorded an old blues number by Arthur 'Big Boy' Crudup: 'That's All Right, Mama'. A few days later, Dewey Phillips – one of the most popular and influential disc jockeys in the area – played the record around 14 times in just one evening

Playing records at June Juanico's house in Biloxi, summer 1956.

Opposite: Music producer Sam Phillips (right) and Bob Neal (left) standing behind Elvis as he signs his management contract with Neal. This was the official picture that ran in the trades – in fact Elvis was still underage so his parents signed for him as his legal guardians.

Previous page: Elvis at around two years old.

(the exact number is uncertain) and told his listeners it was sure to be a hit. The results stunned everybody: thousands of phone calls requested more of the new singer and, much to Sam Phillips's surprise, Elvis's music was not only popular with the white audience, but with the black one too.

At first, Scotty Moore managed the group, but later, DJ Bob Neal took over, making bookings for live appearances at clubs and concerts, and later organizing local concert tours. They began to play regularly at the Eagle's Nest in Memphis, but Sam Phillips also managed to get a booking at that mecca of country singing, Nashville's Grand Ole Opry. It was unheard of for an unknown singer to play the Opry, and all of them were thrilled; unfortunately, though, the audience was not ready for their new style and Elvis was advised to stick to driving trucks. He never played there again. The Louisiana Hayride, broadcast on KWKH from Shreveport's Municipal Auditorium, proved more welcoming. Elvis and the Blue Moon Boys were an instant hit and were quickly invited back. They began to tour almost full-time – often driving all night, playing a concert, then driving on to the next show with just a few snatched hours of sleep in the back of the car. Despite this, Elvis seemed constantly active and rarely tired; when he finally did sleep, though, it would be for 11 or 12 hours.

Now that he was releasing records and playing regularly at the Louisiana Hayride and other well-known venues, Elvis began to feel he was really on his way. He already had a large group of fans who would arrive whenever he was due to appear. He was still a local phenomenon, however, and needed another push to achieve national popularity. That push was not long coming. In late 1954, Elvis met Colonel Tom Parker for the first time, who soon had plans for the still rather naive young singer who was driving audiences wild.

The Colonel had started out in carnival, but moved into showbusiness when he became the manager of singer Eddy Arnold. When he met Elvis, he was working as a promoter, and his astute business practices, promotional skills and attention to detail were already famous. Although his title was an honorary one, conferred by a state governor, he insisted on using it at all times. Having arranged a few tours for Elvis and noting the audience reaction, he began to take over, maneuvering everyone else out of the way.

With the Colonel's help, Elvis transferred to the national stage and was soon headlining shows across the country. Women went wild as he shook his hips or jiggled his legs – movements a world away from those of other singers of the time, who hardly moved at all while they sang. Some religious leaders took exception to his 'lewd' performance, and called for both Elvis and his music to be banned.

At a concert in Jacksonville, Florida, in May 1955, fans rioted, leaping onto the stage and attempting to tear off Elvis's clothes; this soon became a fairly regular occurrence. Elvis loved all the attention and often encouraged his fans – both onstage and off. Despite his polite, shy and humble image, Elvis had a reputation for never turning a woman away from his door. He had been quick to realize that women liked him and that it was easy to persuade them to join him in bed. He dated several different women regularly – even when his steady girlfriend, Dixie Locke, was still waiting for him at home. She eventually split up with him, although not because of the time he spent with his other women; she was dismayed that the demands of touring left him with no time to spend with her.

Gladys had always wanted her son Elvis to be someone special, but now that he was, she found it hard to cope with his fame. He was always away touring instead of at home with her, and she was distressed by the overheated reaction of his female fans. Elvis had been her main emotional support for many years; now he was no longer around and her problems began to escalate.

By November 1955, Colonel Parker had arranged for RCA to buy Elvis's contract from Sam Phillips, who needed funds to develop his other singers – including Johnny Cash, Roy Orbison, Carl Perkins and Jerry Lee Lewis. The following year RCA released its first Elvis single, 'Heartbreak Hotel'. To the disappointment of RCA executives, it was a very different sound to anything Elvis had recorded before and they began to wonder if they had made a costly mistake. However, it was a massive hit, going to No. 1 in the charts and, by mid-1956, Elvis was bringing in over half of RCA's total income.

Elvis also made several appearances on *Stage Show* on CBS TV, reaching an audience across the entire country for the first time. The Colonel soon became Elvis's sole and exclusive manager. He had

recognized that Elvis appealed to a new audience, as the repressed youth of America found their own identity and began to rebel against authority. Naturally, these teenagers wanted their own music, preferably something their elders did not approve of, and rock 'n' roll fitted the bill perfectly. With this audience came a vast new market just waiting to be tapped. Part of Elvis's appeal was that he was a mass of contradictions: he appeared shy and polite but, onstage, moved in a way that drove women crazy; he belted out rock 'n' roll numbers but sang gospel with true feeling; he was quietly spoken and loved his mother, but was also an audacious youth who encouraged teenagers to rebel.

Elvis himself could never understand why there was a problem. He moved the way he did because that was what seemed natural to him; gospel was his own first love, but rock 'n' roll was what the audience wanted; and he never saw himself as a rebel because he had simply grown up with the kind of music he sang. Record sales boomed on the back of all the publicity. The Colonel already had his eye on the next move and, in April 1956, Elvis did a screen test and soon had a movie contract with Paramount Pictures.

Despite everything else that was going on, Elvis was still touring almost non-stop – including a two-week run at the New Frontier Hotel in Las Vegas. Unfortunately, this was not a success as the venue's middle-class audience was more used to sophisticated entertainers like Frank Sinatra and didn't take to the raw energy of Elvis's rock 'n' roll. However, it was in Vegas that Elvis met Liberace, who was to become a close friend, and who advised him on how to dress to please his audience. Elvis's style soon began to change, and he not only solved his skin problems but also had his teeth capped.

Opposite: Elvis demonstrates the leg-shaking action to a fan on stage.

Top: An early poster advertising a concert on a tour through Tennessee, Louisiana, Arkansas, Mississippi and Missouri.

Bottom: On stage not long after 'That's All Right, Mama' was released. Elvis continued to drive a truck for Crown Electric during the day until November 1954.

Don't call us…

The second Sun single, 'Good Rockin'
Tonight' was as great a success as the first.
Elvis, Scotty Moore and Bill Black soon had
regular concert bookings and Sam Phillips
arranged for them to appear on Nashville's
Grand Ole Opry. Unfortunately the
audience was more used to traditional
country singers, and the response was
lukewarm. Afterwards, the show's talent
coordinator, Jim Denny, suggested Elvis
should go back to driving a truck.

In August 1956, Elvis began work on his first movie, *Love Me Tender*, a drama set just after the Civil War. Elvis played the youngest son of a farming family, who marries the girlfriend of his eldest brother after everyone assumes that the brother is dead. When the older brother returns, the family is torn apart and Elvis's character is killed. The movie co-stars Debra Paget and Richard Egan; Elvis appears again at the end, singing the title song over the credits. The Colonel was astute enough to retain the publishing rights to the movie's score, rather than handing them over to the studio, and after Elvis appeared on *The Ed Sullivan Show*, advance orders of two million were received for the single 'Love Me Tender'. The movie opened in 500 theaters that November and was a huge hit, despite an unenthusiastic response from the movie critics.

The Colonel was also quick to realize the potential for Elvis-related merchandize, and set up companies to sell a Presley product range that included jeans, charm bracelets, stick-on sideburns, hair oil, bubblegum cards and even lipstick. At the center of all this fuss, however, Elvis was becoming increasingly isolated, his movements restricted. He was already beginning to acquire the habits that would eventually lead to his destruction.

Elvis appeared for the first time on the Louisiana Hayride in October 1954. This time the performance went down very well and he and the Blue Moon Boys were soon given a contract to appear every Saturday night. The Hayride was broadcast live from the Municipal Auditorium in Shreveport, and reached 28 states; it was much more innovative than the Opry and became a haven for new talent.

The Hillbilly Cat…

Elvis takes a turn at the drums. At first, he was backed on stage only by Scotty on lead guitar and Bill on bass, but after they decided to hire a full-time drummer they were joined by DJ Fontana. As a musician, Elvis was largely self-taught. His parents did not have the money to pay for lessons, but he grew up surrounded by music and quickly learned to carry a tune.

Accomplished pianist

Although he rarely played in public, Elvis was also an accomplished pianist. He usually played for himself or close friends, and only when he felt happy and at ease. He often played gospel music for pleasure and thought about becoming a gospel singer, but rockabilly – the early form of rock 'n' roll – was what the audience wanted.

Elvis Presley

The King of Rock 'n' Roll

After he began to become well known nationally, almost every aspect of Elvis was publicly criticized – his dress, the raunchy way he moved, his ducktail hair, his sideburns. Because of all this negative publicity he soon developed an image as a dangerous rebel, who would encourage young people to defy their elders – but teenagers loved him partly because their elders did disapprove. Elvis himself could never understand the fuss; he did not try to cause offence and almost everyone who met him was soon won over by his quiet, shy charm. The Colonel could see the power of the new teenage market and for a while was content to exploit it – he created all kinds of gimmicks to keep the fans happy and the free publicity also boosted record sales.

After he signed with RCA at the end of 1955, Elvis began to move away from rockabilly into true rock 'n' roll. It was the start of a gradual progression in his style and in his music, always moving on to try and reach a wider audience. How much of this was a natural progression and how much was manipulated by Colonel Parker is open to debate.

Lifelong friends

Elvis first appeared in Las Vegas in April 1956, but the engagement was not a great success. However, he met Liberace there for the first time and the two of them went on to become lifelong friends.

Speculating about romance

Judy Powell Spreckels, former wife of sugar heir Adolph Spreckels, manages to catch Elvis after *The Milton Berle Show*. The two of them exchanged rings, and the press speculated that they were enjoying a romance.

Opposite: The Milton Berle Show that featured Elvis's first appearance was broadcast from the deck of the USS *Hancock*, which was docked at the San Diego Naval Station. Despite the novelty of the location, it was his second appearance on the show in June of that year that brought more publicity.

Hound Dog

During his second appearance on *The Milton Berle Show*, Elvis sang 'Hound Dog' for the first time on television. It was a new song, but the audience loved it and Elvis responded to their enthusiasm by taking his hip-swivelling performance to greater heights. 'Hound Dog' was released in July 1956 and sold over five million copies by the end of the year.

Topping the ratings

As he reached the final part of 'Hound Dog', Elvis slowed down the tempo of the song and proceeded to thrust his hips in time to the music in a distinctly suggestive way. The studio audience were driven to a frenzy of excitement, screaming and laughing at the same time. That evening, for the first time in the season, *The Milton Berle Show* topped *Sergeant Bilko* in the ratings.

Fans furious at critics' response

Soon afterwards Elvis appeared on the *Steve Allen Show*, but Allen insisted his performance be toned down and that he should wear a tuxedo. The fans were furious, and picketed the NBC studios the following morning.

Opposite: The day after *The Milton Berle Show* was broadcast, many critics condemned Elvis's performance. John Crosby of the *New York Herald Tribune* said he was 'unspeakably untalented and vulgar', Jack O'Brian of the New York Journal-American wrote of '…a display of primitive physical movement difficult to describe in terms suitable to a family newspaper…', and Ben Gross said in the Daily News that '…he gave an exhibition that was suggestive and vulgar, tinged with the kind of animalism that should be confined to dives and bordellos.'

A new, confident Elvis

On stage at Russwood Park, in July 1956. When Elvis first appeared, dressed all in black except for red socks and tie, the fans rushed out of their seats and swept forwards towards the stage. The last few months had given Elvis a new confidence, so he was able to tease and control the crowd without letting anything get out of hand.

Time out for Mom and Dad

Top: Elvis takes time out to have a few words with his mother, Gladys, and father, Vernon.

Bottom: The Colonel always had a supply of photographs for the fans to buy – and Elvis was happy to sign them. In later years, he rarely went out in public because he was constantly mobbed by his fans.

Hollywood, here I come

In August 1956, filming began on Elvis's first movie, *Love Me Tender*, which was being made by Twentieth-Century Fox. After his screen test for Hal Wallis, Elvis had been offered a three-picture deal by Paramount – but they had no suitable vehicle for him, so had loaned him to Twentieth-Century Fox. Elvis had an excellent memory, and he not only knew his own part before he arrived in Hollywood, but had also learned the entire script by heart. His co-stars were Richard Egan and Debra Paget, both experienced actors, and Elvis was very nervous but also extremely willing to learn. The producer, David Weisbart, had produced *Rebel Without a Cause* and Elvis was excited to meet him as he had deeply admired James Dean.

Down on the farm…

Originally entitled *The Reno Brothers*, *Love Me Tender* was a drama, set just after the Civil War. Elvis played the youngest son of a farming family, who marries the girlfriend of his eldest brother after everyone assumes that the brother is dead. When the older brother returns, the family is torn apart and Elvis's character is killed. Since the producers worried that the fans would be upset if their idol died, an alternative ending was shot, in which he survives. In the end they stayed with the original storyline, but Elvis appears again at the end, singing the title song over the credits.

Love Me Tender: a million orders

The theme song, 'Love Me Tender', was based on a Civil War ballad called 'Aura Lee'. Elvis was better known for more raunchy numbers, but he sang the ballad with real feeling. When it was released in September 1956 as a single the song was a great hit, so the name of the movie was quickly changed to *Love Me Tender* before it was released. This was the only movie in which Elvis appeared where the part was not specifically written for him – in fact Robert Wagner was originally under consideration to play the role.

Time revealed that RCA had record-breaking advance orders of one million for the single, and even before the movie opened the record reached No. 1 in the *Billboard* Top 100.

Natural acting ability

Producer David Weisbart told reporters that Elvis had the same smoldering appeal for teenagers, and the same impulsive nature, as James Dean. He advised Elvis not to have acting lessons but to rely on his greatest asset – his natural ability.

Opposite top: Debra Paget played the elder brother's girlfriend in *Love Me Tender*. Elvis had a big crush on her, but she did not return his regard – although she thought he was 'very sweet'.

Opposite bottom: Although *Love Me Tender* had only four musical numbers, they were carefully worked into the storyline.

Charming the birds from the trees…

Elvis was well-liked by his co-stars, and they went out of their way to help him in the new and strange world of movie-making. Richard Egan, who played the elder brother, said of him later, 'That boy could charm the birds from the trees'.

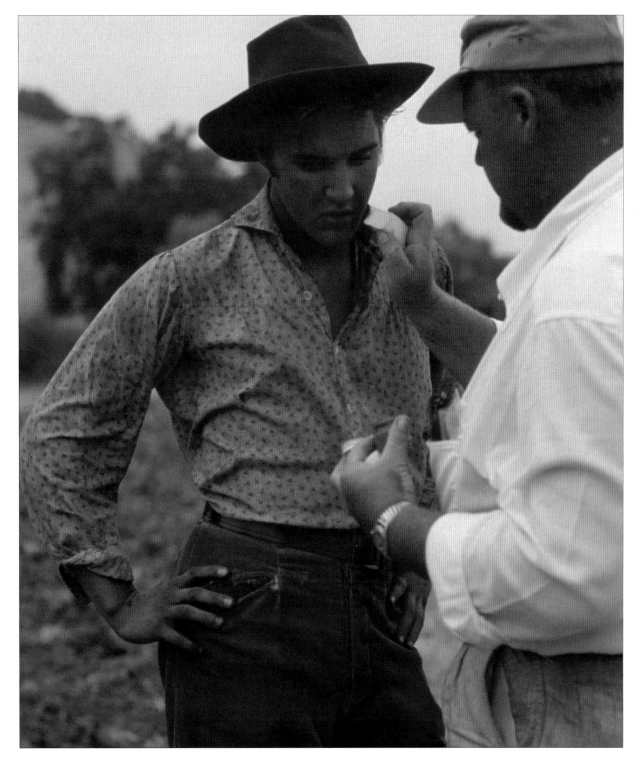

Director Robert Webb was very patient with his fledgling star, taking him aside between shots to go over the scenes and breaking the lines down to show the emphasis.

Back home in Tupelo

Nick Adams, an actor and Hollywood hustler who had become Elvis's friend, introduced him to Natalie Wood. The papers reported that Elvis and Natalie were having a sizzling romance, but they usually went around in a gang with Nick and his other friends. Natalie described Elvis as 'a real pixie… he has a wonderful little-boy quality'.

Opposite: In September, Elvis appeared at a homecoming concert back in Tupelo. Before the concert began a parade was held in his honor, but the Colonel vetoed the suggestion that Elvis should ride in it because of concerns over security. Main Street was decked with a giant banner that said, 'Tupelo Welcomes Elvis Presley Home'. Elvis's parents, Vernon and Gladys, were there to see his triumph – though Gladys later told a friend that it had made her uncomfortable to remember how poor they had been when they lived there.

He wore Blue Velvet

For the concert, Elvis wore a heavy blue velvet shirt that Natalie Wood had had made for him by her own tailor – despite the fact that it was a very hot day. He teased the crowd, walking close to the edge of the stage and leaning down so the fans could just touch his fingers. One time he misjudged the distance, and lost one of the silver buttons from his shirt.

During the concert, Tupelo mayor James Ballard gave Elvis the key to the city and Mississippi governor JP Coleman came on stage to praise 'America's number-one entertainer'.

On second thoughts…

Ed Sullivan discusses a few points with Elvis during preparations for his second appearance on *The Ed Sullivan Show* in October 1956. Although Sullivan had declared that Elvis would never appear on his show, he later backed down and signed him for three performances. Elvis was paid a total of $50,000 for his appearances – which was considerably more than the sum the Colonel had originally asked for when he first approached Sullivan and had been turned down. When the first show was broadcast in early September, actor Charles Laughton acted as host since Sullivan was recovering from a car accident.

Fooling with Bill Black

While Elvis played to the girls, Bill Black often played the fool with his bass in the background. Sometimes he pretended to dance with it, at others he rode it like horse – which always elicited a laugh from the audience. The ratings for the *Sullivan Show* – and every other show – invariably went up when Elvis appeared.

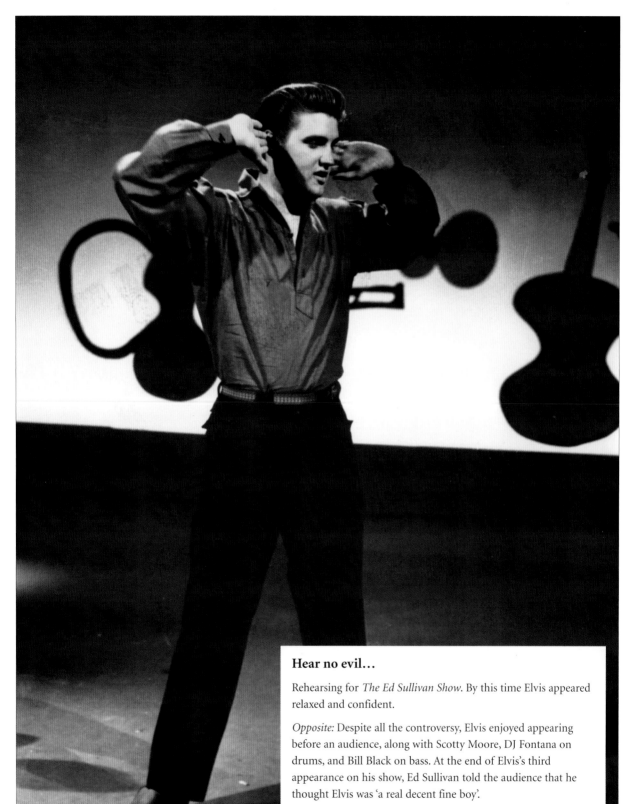

Hear no evil…

Rehearsing for *The Ed Sullivan Show*. By this time Elvis appeared relaxed and confident.

Opposite: Despite all the controversy, Elvis enjoyed appearing before an audience, along with Scotty Moore, DJ Fontana on drums, and Bill Black on bass. At the end of Elvis's third appearance on his show, Ed Sullivan told the audience that he thought Elvis was 'a real decent fine boy'.

Star guest

Liberace talking to Elvis in the audience on the opening night of his concert at the Hotel Riviera in Las Vegas. Elvis was taking a few days off in Vegas, staying at the New Frontier Hotel.

Opposite: Elvis and June Juanico, whom he had first met in her home town of Biloxi when he had played the Keesler Air Force Base in 1955. Almost a year later they met again in Memphis and dated for several months through the summer of 1956.

Just pure gold

After the concert, Liberace and Elvis swopped jackets and instruments and fooled around for the cameras. Liberace's jacket was a gold cutaway, and was the inspiration for the famous $2,500 gold-lamé suit that the Colonel had made up for Elvis by Nudie Cohen the following year. Liberace told journalists, 'Elvis and I may be characters – but we can afford to be.' Elvis always sent flowers for Liberace's opening nights.

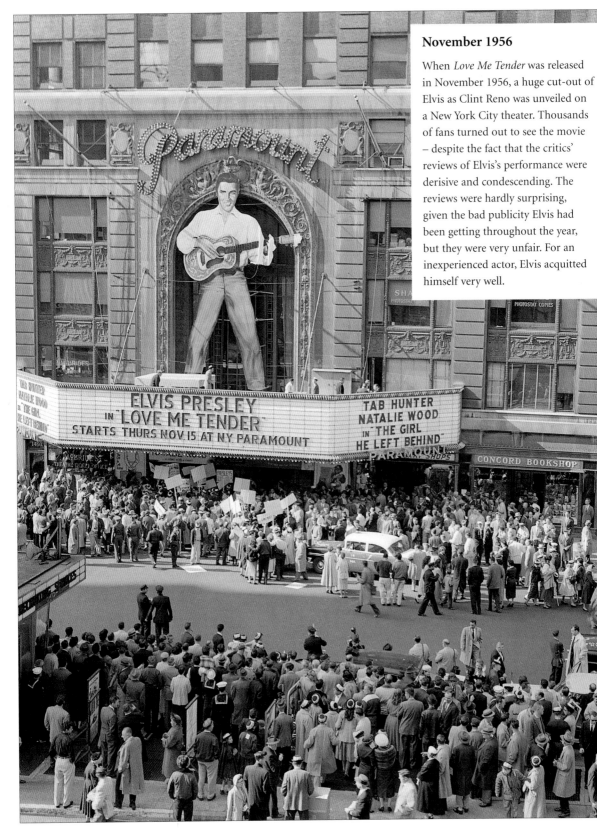

November 1956

When *Love Me Tender* was released in November 1956, a huge cut-out of Elvis as Clint Reno was unveiled on a New York City theater. Thousands of fans turned out to see the movie – despite the fact that the critics' reviews of Elvis's performance were derisive and condescending. The reviews were hardly surprising, given the bad publicity Elvis had been getting throughout the year, but they were very unfair. For an inexperienced actor, Elvis acquitted himself very well.

MR. ROCK 'N' ROLL IN THE STORY HE WAS BORN TO PLAY!

Love Him Strong!
Love Him Sweet!
Love Him Tender!

The great adventure of the notorious Reno Brothers— and the girl they fought for!

HE'S A FIGHTIN' MAN... as Clint, youngest of the notorious Reno Brothers!

HE'S A SINGIN' MAN... singin' 'Love Me Tender'...'We're Gonna Move'...'Poor Boy'...'Let Me!'

HE'S A LOVIN' MAN... who loved his brother but also loved his brother's girl!

20th CENTURY-FOX presents

RICHARD EGAN · DEBRA PAGET
and introducing **ELVIS PRESLEY** in

LOVE ME TENDER
A CINEMASCOPE PICTURE

co-starring ROBERT MIDDLETON · WILLIAM CAMPBELL · NEVILLE BRAND with MILDRED DUNNOCK, BRUCE BENNETT

Produced by DAVID WEISBART · Directed by ROBERT D. WEBB · Screenplay by ROBERT BUCKNER · Based on a Story by MAURICE GERAGHTY

A casual, windswept Elvis. By the end of 1956, he had come a long way. His records were now in the charts, he had a nationwide following of fans and had made his first Hollywood movie, which was a big box office success. Despite all the adulation, most people agree that in terms of his character he had changed very little. He was still unfailing polite and charming to everyone he met, and he still went home to his parents whenever he had the opportunity. However, the obsessive behavior of the fans was becoming an increasing problem – Elvis could hardly walk down the street without getting besieged by adoring admirers.

Car-crazy…

Below: The former truck driver studies the engine of something a little more powerful. Throughout his life Elvis had a fascination for cars and he not only bought many for himself, he also often bought them as gifts for friends, acquaintances – and even total strangers. The first car he ever owned was a 1941 Lincoln coupé, bought by Vernon and Gladys. When he first began to earn serious money he bought his mother a brand new pink Cadillac – even though she did not drive.

Left: A relaxed Elvis in front of the camera.

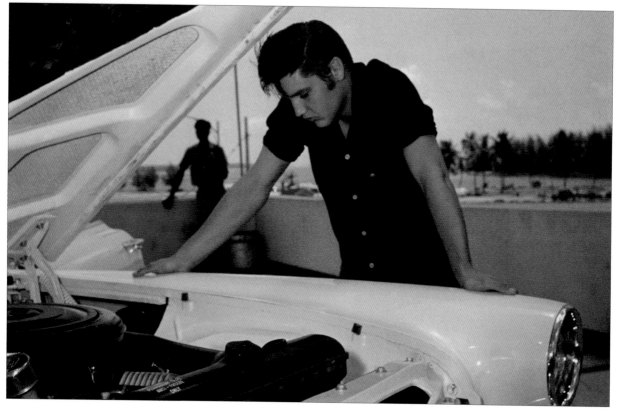

Chapter Two

Treat Me Nice

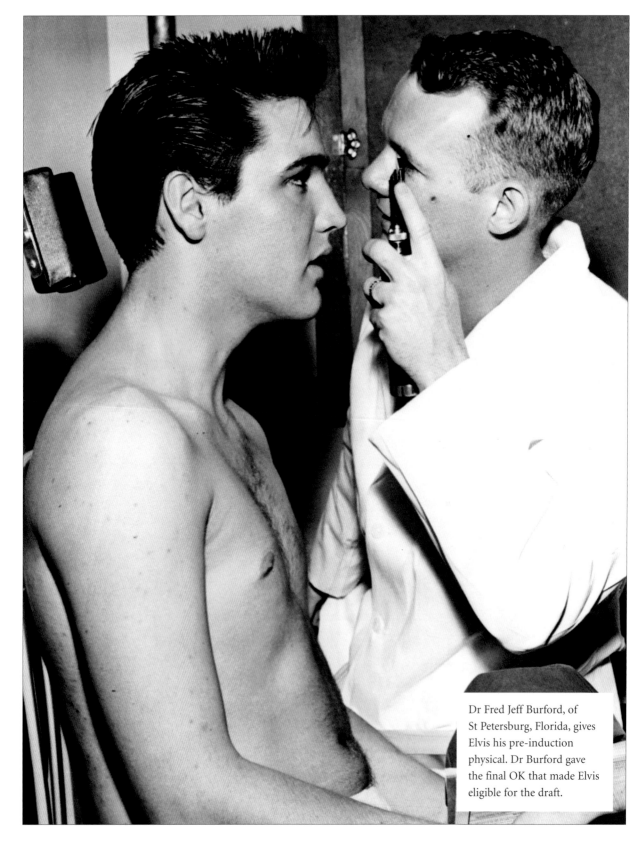

Dr Fred Jeff Burford, of
St Petersburg, Florida, gives
Elvis his pre-induction
physical. Dr Burford gave
the final OK that made Elvis
eligible for the draft.

By the beginning of 1957, Elvis was accompanied by armed security guards wherever he went, since he could no longer so much as step into the street without being mobbed by fans, causing a riot. He was constantly surrounded by members of his entourage, a close-knit circle of men who were both companions and support group. They fuelled his ego, rushed to fulfil every whim, and were on hand 24 hours a day to sing gospel or to party. Often badly behaved, they appeared arrogant to outsiders, and they soon became known in most circles as the 'Memphis Mafia'.

After Elvis had played a concert, he and the Mafia would usually party all night with local musicians – and plenty of girls too. To relax, he sang gospel music or played the piano. He could now afford to buy whatever he wanted to eat – but had a weakness for junk food, particularly cheeseburgers, sliced banana and peanut butter sandwiches, greasy doughnuts, crisply burnt bacon, fried or mashed potatoes and dark-brown gravy. A diet of this kind of food was beginning to cause weight problems – although he was still burning off a great many calories in nervous energy. He also often walked in his sleep when he was anxious or upset, which gave those around him cause for concern about his safety. During the unhappy booking at the New Frontier Hotel in Las Vegas in 1956, his companion Red West regularly sat up all night in case Elvis walked straight out of the open window.

Despite Elvis's burgeoning health problems, the hours spent on the road, the constant lack of sleep and his poor diet, he always seemed to find plenty of energy when it was time to take the stage.

For some time, rumours had been spreading that Elvis was about to be drafted. Early in 1957 he reported to the Kennedy Veterans Hospital in Memphis for his pre-induction US Army physical; he was classed 1-A and therefore eligible for military service, although the authorities said it was unlikely he would be called within the next six months. The Army also confirmed that the famous hair – Elvis's pride and joy – would have to come off. Meanwhile, there was another film to be made, *Loving You*, about a singer in search of fame. It also starred Lizbeth Scott and Wendell Corey – established actors who would not feel the need to eclipse the new kid on the block. Gladys and Vernon came to visit their son on-set and were filmed for one scene, watching the concert that takes place at the climax of the story.

One of the first major purchases Elvis had made with his new-found wealth was a home for his parents, in Audubon Drive, Memphis. Unfortunately, fans often turned up in their hundreds to hang around outside, and the neighbours soon tired of this constant intrusion. Elvis decided he needed a property with some seclusion, so Vernon and Gladys set out to find one. As soon as they saw Graceland they fell in love with it, and quickly called Elvis to come and see it for himself. A Georgian colonial-style mansion, Graceland had been built in 1939 for Dr Thomas Moore and his wife, and named after Mrs Moore's great aunt Grace, who had owned the land. It was set in 13.75 acres of grounds, and placed well back from Highway 51 – later to be renamed Elvis Presley Boulevard. Elvis was immediately enthusiastic about the property, and the purchase was completed within a week. Renovations were soon under way, as well as essential structural repairs. Elvis had a swimming pool added, and installed a real soda fountain and specially made gates with a musical note motif. He had the interior entirely redecorated, mostly in dark colours with glitzy touches. Over the years, further additions included a recording studio, a 40-foot trophy room, stables, fenced-in fields and vegetable gardens.

His mother was very happy at the idea of moving in and wanted her own chicken house and hog pen, but things did not turn out quite the way she expected. She soon missed the company and the casual get-togethers that had been a major part of her life in town, and began to feel increasingly isolated. Elvis was constantly touring or filming, and Vernon seemed to be busy much of the time. Even when Elvis was there, he was constantly surrounded by other people, as Graceland had also become home to various members of the Memphis Mafia and to a changing population of band members, back-up singers and starlets. This meant that Gladys had little time alone with her son.

Although Elvis continued to perform regularly, it was becoming somewhat hazardous to attend his concerts because of the wild behavior of some of the fans – and even he couldn't hear himself sing over the noise they made. There was also growing discontent in his backing group, as Bill Black, Scotty Moore and drummer DJ Fontana were still only being paid a flat rate of $200 a week when they were working, with a retainer of $100 a week when they were not. Since they were by no means working full-time but, at the same time, were banned from appearing other than with Elvis, their incomes were severely limited. DJ had come in later than the others and had always been a salaried employee so he was relatively content, but the Blue Moon Boys had been with Elvis from the beginning and felt they deserved better. Apart from the money problem, they were bored in Hollywood, where they had little to do, and found they were increasingly being excluded from direct contact with Elvis himself.

Shooting was soon to begin on another movie, *Jailhouse Rock*, in which Elvis plays a bad boy who reforms in prison and goes on to become a famous singing star. It was one of his best movies, with specially commissioned songs by Leiber and Stoller,

who came out to Hollywood to oversee the recording. Unfortunately, one of the Colonel's stipulations in his management of Elvis was to make sure that the writers of his songs handed over a percentage of their royalties. Word of this soon got around, seriously limiting the selection of songs Elvis was offered in later years – to the point that it began to damage his career.

During rehearsals for the opening dance sequence in *Jailhouse Rock*, a porcelain cap came off one of Elvis's teeth and he managed to inhale it. The cap lodged in one of his lungs and he was taken to the hospital, where doctors managed to retrieve it by inserting an instrument via his vocal cords and down into the lung. Elvis was hoarse for a few days afterwards, but to everyone's relief, his voice soon recovered.

Elvis got along very well with Judy Tyler, his co-star in *Jailhouse Rock*, but, being newly married, she wasn't interested in any sort of romantic attachment with him. Tragically, she and her husband were killed in a car accident soon after filming finished, and Elvis was so upset he could never watch the finished picture. Another important relationship hit the rocks in this period. The DJ Dewey Phillips, who had first played 'That's All Right, Mama' and been so instrumental in launching Elvis's career, came out to visit him in Hollywood. Elvis played him a single that was about to be released, 'Teddy Bear', from his previous movie, *Loving You*. Phillips loved it and, against Elvis's explicit instructions, took a copy of the record and played it on air on his return to Memphis. Because the record had not even been released, Phillips' scoop infuriated both the Colonel and record executives, and Elvis and Phillips had a major falling-out. Although they were later to patch things up, their friendship was never quite the same.

Back in Memphis, Elvis began dating Anita Wood, a blonde former beauty queen whom he had

Las Vegas dancer Dorothy Harmony accompanied Elvis to his pre-induction physical in February 1958. He had met Dorothy during his first appearance in Vegas the previous year and they had been dating regularly since. She had spent two weeks with the Presley family in Memphis over Christmas and the photographs of her opening her presents with the family precipitated his split with June Juanico.

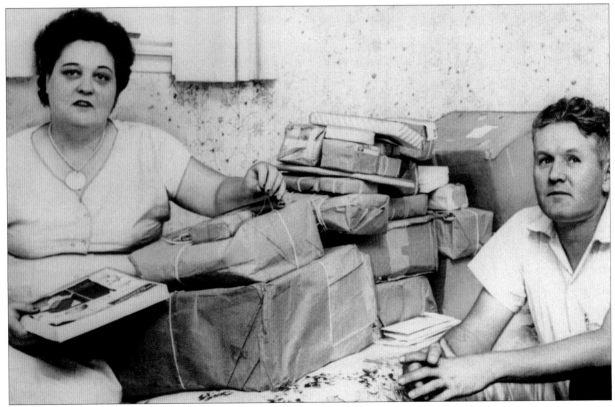

Art follows life…

The storyline of Elvis's second movie, *Loving You*, was loosely based on his own life. Elvis played Deke Rivers, an unknown but talented singer with a new sound. Lizabeth Scott, a hard-headed music promoter, exploits him for his appeal to teenage audiences but the press soon label him as a bad influence and a rebel. After Deke manages to convince people that he is really a fine, upstanding young man, the movie ends happily.

Opposite top: Although here it is in pristine condition, Elvis's cars were often defaced by his female fans, who were so desperate to meet him that they wrote their telephone numbers and messages in lipstick all over the paint work.

Opposite bottom: Gladys and Vernon are pictured with just a few of the hundreds of gifts from fans that Elvis received on his 22nd birthday. The fans often gathered outside his parents' home in Memphis and the neighbors were beginning to get annoyed with the constant intrusions.

Proud owner of Graceland

The new owner of Graceland stands proudly
next to one of the columns of the entrance
portico. The renovations and decorations
that Elvis wanted were to cost almost as
much again as the house itself – and one of
his priorities was to create 'the most beautiful
bedroom in Memphis' for his mother.

Opposite bottom: One of the new additions
Elvis made to Graceland was the installation
of a pair of custom-made gates with a
musical motif.

All Shook Up

Elvis and Dolores Hart share a joke on the set of *Loving You* filmed in the early part of 1957. Elvis had his hair dyed black for the part, and it looked so well he continued to dye it for the rest of his life. Its natural color was more a dark blonde. In April of that year, 'All Shook Up' reached No. 1 on the *Billboard* Top 100 and stayed there for eight weeks.

In trouble…

Top: Elvis got himself into trouble when he was accused of pulling a gun on a Private First Class Hershel, after the young Marine claimed Elvis had insulted his wife. Since Elvis had never met Mrs Hershel – and the gun was a prop, which he had brought back from Hollywood – the whole affair was settled out of court.

Bottom: In a still from his third movie, *Jailhouse Rock*, Elvis plays Vince Everett, who is sent to prison for killing a man in self-defence. His character is hot-blooded and bitter over the unfair sentence, and becomes an angry, sullen and brooding young man. The fans are therefore treated to several scenes of a very passionate and provocative Elvis.

Opposite: Jailhouse Rock was a low-budget movie shot in black and white, with stylized sets, but the simple settings enhanced the serious storyline. Many believe it was one of the best movies Elvis ever made – and it made a great deal of money for MGM and for Elvis himself, who received a large percentage of the profits.

1957: Jailhouse Rock

For the big dance sequence performed to the title song, Elvis was backed by a team of professional dancers. He had initially been wary about the whole idea, but choreographer Alex Romero watched Elvis move around naturally when he was singing, and then worked the steps up into a routine. Elvis was much more comfortable and enthusiastic with the final result, and it looks very like the way he normally moved on stage. The single 'Jailhouse Rock'/'Treat Me Nice' was also a great success and sold over three million copies in 12 months in the US. It was the first Elvis record to reach No. 1 in the charts in Britain.

Bad boy image

Top: Jailhouse Rock played on Elvis's bad boy image. While Vince Everett is in jail, he learns to sing and play the guitar from another inmate. Afterwards Vince becomes a famous rock star, but is not a particularly pleasant person until an accident stops him in his tracks. He becomes a nice guy who falls in love with the heroine, Peggy van Alden, played by Judy Tyler.

Bottom: Elvis and Anne Neyland, a former Miss Texas who also appeared in *Jailhouse Rock,* exchange a smoldering look. They dated during the shooting of the movie and for a few weeks afterwards.

Opposite: Elvis threw himself into the dance routine with such abandon that he swallowed one of the temporary caps from his teeth. It lodged in his lung and had to be recovered with surgery. For a while there was some concern that Elvis's voice would be affected, but the fears proved to be groundless.

True love in the movies

Judy Tyler, as Peggy van Alden, watches Vince during one of the scenes from *Jailhouse Rock*. Peggy is the record promoter who helps Vince to stardom and falls in love with him – but haughtily refuses to respond to his advances until he becomes a reformed man.

Devastated by Judy's death

Elvis and Judy were great friends during the shooting of the movie – but Judy was newly married and not interested in romance. A few weeks after shooting finished, she and her husband were killed in a car accident. Elvis was devastated and did not attend the movie's premiere.

Parting is such sweet sorrow…

Anita Wood hugs Elvis goodbye, as he prepares to
leave on a whirlwind tour of the Pacific northwest.
Anita was a former beauty queen, who was now
appearing on *Top Ten Dance Party* on WHBQ.
She had just won the Mid-South Hollywood Star
Hunt and was also about to leave, for the finalists'
competition in New Orleans. The two of them
were together for several years – although that
didn't stop Elvis from dating a number of other
women during the same period.

Elvis's tour…

The tour covered five cities in four days, so there was little time for rest and relaxation. Elvis and Tom Diskin, his road manager, were accompanied by George Klein, Lamar Fike and Cliff Gleaves. By this stage, Elvis had a string of hits including 'All Shook Up, 'Teddy Bear' and 'Jailhouse Rock' which were all released during 1957.

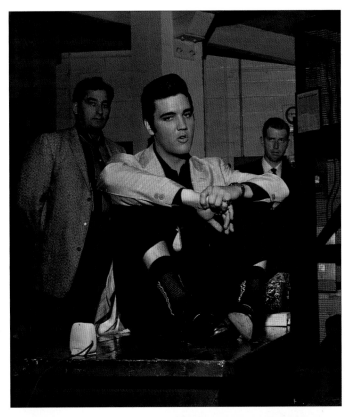

Causing a riot on tour

During the tour there were riots in nearly every city, and in Spokane, Washington, fans broke onto the infield of the Memorial Stadium and tried to steal the soil because Elvis's feet had touched it. In Vancouver, a contingent of Canadian Mounties had been drafted in to hold back the crowd of 25,000, but they were quickly overwhelmed. The Colonel pulled Elvis offstage and the fans were told to get back to their seats before he would continue. Elvis couldn't resist teasing the crowd again, and the concert was stopped for a second time. Finally they managed to proceed, but at the end Elvis was whisked away as fans engulfed the stage, grabbing everything they could get their hands on.

Left: After the concert in Vancouver, the paper's music critic, Dr Ida Halpern, described his performance as 'subsidized sex'.

Below: Elvis studies his reviews. He now ended every show with 'Hound Dog', which he introduced as the 'Elvis Presley national anthem'. After the tour was over he was scheduled to go on to a recording session organized by RCA, to lay down tracks for a special Christmas album.

A professional touch…

During the filming of *Jailhouse Rock* Elvis became friendly with professional dancer Russ Tamblyn, who gave him a few tips to sharpen up his dancing style.

ELVIS
IN
ACTION
AS
NEVER
BEFORE !

Millionaire mover with MGM deal

After *Jailhouse Rock* was released nationwide,
the Colonel estimated that he and Elvis were
due to make more than two million dollars
through their percentage deal with MGM.

Screaming and swooning

The fans now made so much noise during the concerts that no one could hear Elvis sing. They even screamed and swooned while just watching him on the screen.

Below: The Memphis premiere of *Jailhouse Rock* was held in the theater where Elvis had once worked briefly as an usher.

ELVIS PRESLEY

JAILHOUSE ROCK

JUDY TYLER

RICHARD THORPE PANDRO S. BER

Drafted!

Just before Christmas 1957, Elvis received his draft notification and although he collected the notice himself to avoid publicity, the press soon got wind of it. He told reporters that he was happy the situation was finally resolved and that he was happy to return something to the country that had given him so much. When photographers wanted to picture him with the notice a minor panic ensued, as Elvis couldn't remember where he had put it.

Chapter Three

It's Now or Never

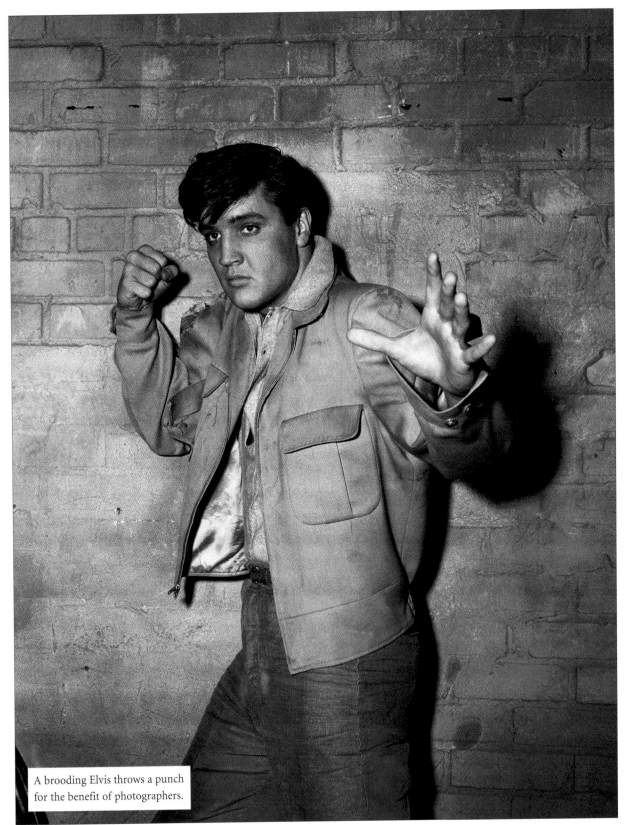

A brooding Elvis throws a punch for the benefit of photographers.

Early in January 1958, Elvis flew to California to record the soundtrack for *King Creole* and then begin filming. The film told the story of a young man who dropped out of college and became involved with gangsters, but then overcame adversity to become a famous singer. It had some similarities with Elvis's life and was one of the few of his own films that he liked. Both the director, Michael Curtiz, and Elvis's co-star, Walter Matthau (who played the heavy), were impressed with how Elvis approached the role, and believed he would go on to become a great actor. Elvis himself was determined to do his best, as it might be his last film. Who knew what would happen when he returned from the Army?

Two weeks after shooting had finished, Elvis was finally inducted into the US Army. He turned up early at the draft board, accompanied by Anita Wood, and various friends and relatives, to be greeted by the Colonel and a group of journalists and photographers from the press. After a short media interview, Elvis was taken off to the Kennedy Veterans Hospital with his fellow recruits to be checked out, but even his medical examination was conducted in the glare of publicity. The bus taking Elvis on to Fort Chaffee, Arkansas, was followed by hundreds of cars and, at a scheduled stop for coffee and sandwiches, there were so many people already waiting that no one was able to leave the bus. The commander in charge at Fort Chaffee had agreed that the press would have full access, so Elvis made his bed for the cameras, had breakfast with the Colonel and newsmen, and was photographed having his hair cut, and being issued with and wearing his uniform. He was assigned to the Second Armored Division at Fort Hood in Texas for basic training, where he was also to receive advanced tank instruction. Having seen the circus around Fort Chaffee, those in charge at Fort Hood decided to take a different approach. The media were given one day of free access, after which the new recruit was strictly off-limits. It was the first time Elvis had been on his own, away from his family and friends. Although he was homesick, he kept his feelings to himself and buckled down to learning how to be a soldier. After some initial difficulties, the other soldiers eventually accepted him as one of the boys.

The Colonel discovered that a soldier could live off base after basic training if he had dependants in the area. So Vernon and Gladys quickly packed up and moved to Killeen, the nearest town to the base. At first they lived in a trailer, but since Vernon's mother, Minnie Presley, and one of the Memphis Mafia, Lamar Fike, had come with them, they soon found a house to rent instead. Elvis drove back and forth to the base each day, and at weekends Anita often came to stay.

Everything seemed to be progressing smoothly, but Gladys was feeling increasingly ill and the hot Texas summer wasn't helping. In August she decided to return to Memphis to see her doctor, who rushed her off to hospital. Despite many tests it was unclear exactly what the problem was, but it was certainly serious and Elvis was called. He was initially unable to get leave, but after threatening to go AWOL was given a pass on compassionate grounds. Although she appeared to rally when Elvis appeared, Gladys died of a heart attack two days later.

Elvis was inconsolable, and not embarrassed to show it. He and his father wept openly, and Elvis told the press that his mother's death had broken his heart. They had been so close, despite the time they had spent apart over the last few years while he had been building his career; she had been the one person he could always trust to be there for him. Her body was laid out at Graceland so that friends and relatives could pay their last respects. Elvis couldn't stop touching her, patting her hands, kissing her and pleading with her to come back. Those close to him eventually talked him away and he was given a sedative to help him sleep. At the funeral, Elvis almost collapsed, and old friends rallied round to help him get through the next few days, but just over a week after his mother's death he had to return to Fort Hood and the Army.

There were several more weeks of training to get through, and Elvis was a diligent recruit and managed well despite his grief. The following month, his unit was transferred by train to New York, where it was to join the ship that would take it to Germany. Elvis's embarkation was marked by the usual media circus – at a press conference he answered questions about the Army, marriage, his mother and his music, and was photographed going up the gangplank with a borrowed duffel bag. Elvis was not going abroad alone, though – he had arranged for Vernon, his grandmother, and Memphis Mafia members Lamar Fike and Red West to come over separately and set up home near his base. The Colonel was to stay behind in America to make sure 'his boy' was not forgotten while he was away.

Although he had never been abroad before – let alone toured there – Elvis was greeted by thousands of ecstatic fans when his ship docked at Bremerhaven. His unit transferred by train to Friedberg, where he was to spend his service, and after a press conference in the canteen, all media were banned from the US base. A day later, Elvis's entourage arrived in the country, and after renting rooms in a couple of hotels for several months, settled in a rented house at Goethestrasse 14, which became Elvis's home when he was not on duty for the rest of the time he was in Germany.

Although Elvis did the usual soldier's duties and went on maneuvers while in the Army, he had an easier life than many soldiers. Lamar and Red looked after his uniform for him, and he had enough money to buy spare kit, so he always looked smart. During several of his leaves, he and his friends travelled to Paris, where they visited famous nightclubs such as the Folies Bergère, the Lido and the Moulin Rouge, and the showgirls were always ready to party.

Elvis dated several German girls while he was in their country, but there were no serious relationships. He was still seeing Anita, and she came over to visit him several times. However, at a club in Wiesbaden in November 1959, he was introduced to Priscilla Beaulieu. The step-daughter of an Army officer, Priscilla was only 14, but was very pretty and Elvis enjoyed her company. They saw each other regularly during the rest of the time he was there, and

he met her parents, but since he was also still seeing other women, their relationship was by no means exclusive. Vernon also met someone – Dee Stanley, the wife of a sergeant and mother of three young boys. She and Vernon soon began an affair, which deeply upset Elvis since it was only just over a year since his beloved mother had died.

Meanwhile the Colonel was keeping things going in America. Before he left, Elvis had recorded several songs, so there were still some records to release in his absence. The Colonel also made sure there was a steady stream of stories in the press about Elvis and his Army career – complete with a few pictures of him looking handsome in uniform. He sent out messages on Elvis's behalf and made sure the fans were kept satisfied; although he was careful not to flood the market so that they would still want more. He was so successful that more than one million

Elvis celebrating his 23rd birthday, with a little help from two of his friends. His celebration that year was low-key, as his imminent induction into the Army had put everyone in low spirits.

Opposite: Carolyn Jones, as the mobster's girlfriend, takes an interest in singer Danny Fisher, played by Elvis, in a scene from *King Creole*.

advance orders for any record Elvis cared to make on his return had already been received, and several new movie projects were agreed.

In March 1960, after two years, Elvis's Army career was finally drawing to a close. He had been promoted twice, and now held the rank of sergeant – although pictures taken on his return show his uniform with an extra stripe, denoting the rank of staff sergeant, which he did not earn. Before he left Germany, Priscilla came to bid him a tearful farewell and he promised to call her, but she was not certain she would ever see him again. Back in America, as he went through the motions of being discharged, the media circus began to gear up again, with coverage of him receiving his final pay check – and immediately handing it over to the Colonel – waving to crowds in his uniform, and the journey back home to Graceland.

Most people agree that his time in the service changed Elvis – afterwards he was more mature and conservative professionally, and his music became more mainstream. However, there was also another and more serious change. According to several people who knew him at the time, Elvis had started to take amphetamines regularly. Apparently, he had first used them to help him stay awake during night maneuvers in Germany, but now took them on a daily basis – not only to keep him going but to help him stay thin. He had come out of the Army 15 pounds lighter than when he went in, but still tended to prefer junk food. Throughout his life, he strongly disapproved of drug-taking, but since the amphetamines were prescription drugs, he did not regard them in the same light. The pills not only caused unpredictable mood swings, but also contributed to Elvis's growing disconnection from the normal world.

One of the first things the Colonel had lined up for his return was an appearance on a Frank Sinatra special, which was to be taped at the Fountainbleau Hotel in Miami Beach. Elvis caught a train down to Florida, and the track was lined with people for almost its entire length – his fans had not forgotten

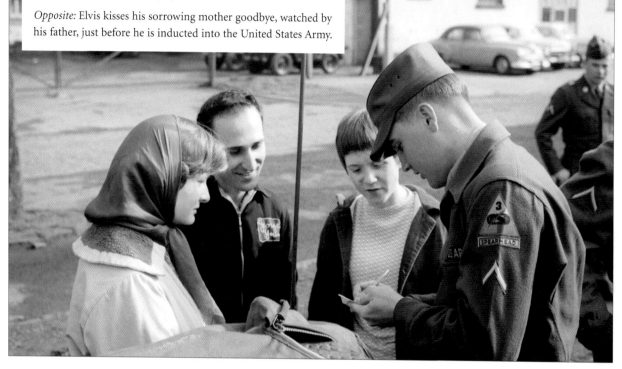

Two teenagers visiting the US 3rd Armored Division's Open House at Ray Barracks in Friedberg, Germany are lucky enough to get Elvis's autograph. Elvis was on duty explaining the various items of equipment on his jeep to visitors.

Opposite: Elvis kisses his sorrowing mother goodbye, watched by his father, just before he is inducted into the United States Army.

him. After the show, he went back to the studio to record new songs, and then to begin the soundtrack for a new movie, *GI Blues*. The movie's storyline was lightweight and capitalized on Elvis's time in the Army. His character was a soldier who also happens to be a musician, who falls in love with a cabaret singer. It was set in Germany, but all of Elvis's scenes were shot in Hollywood. It marked a change from his previous movies in that he was no longer playing a bad boy who makes good, but a safe and wholesome character. He also completed another western, *Flaming Star*, in 1960, and began shooting *Wild in the Country*, both for Twentieth Century Fox. These movies allowed him to move away from his singing a little and tackle slightly more dramatic roles.

The Sinatra show was broadcast in May 1960, and the audience was split between those who loved

Elvis's new, mature, laid-back style, and those who wondered where the rebel rocker had gone. The doubters were heavily outnumbered, though. Elvis lost few fans and picked up many more, so he was still one of the most popular singers in America.

At home, however, things were not so happy. Dee had divorced her former husband, and she and Vernon finally got married, although Elvis refused to go to their wedding. The newlyweds moved into Graceland with Dee's three sons for a while, but soon moved out again into a place of their own.

As he settled back into his old life, Elvis was still dating Anita, but he was also seeing several other women on a casual basis. Despite her doubts, he did call Priscilla regularly, and they talked about her coming over to America to see him. It was not to happen for another two years.

March 1958: You're in the Army now…

Opposite: Major Elbert P Turner swears Elvis into the Army at the draft board in Memphis, Tennessee. The new recruit told reporters that he was dreading the haircut he would get the following day, but that he hoped he would be treated the same as everyone else.

Left: Elvis's induction into the Army had been deferred so he could complete filming on *King Creole*. The story was of a young singer, Danny Fisher – played by Elvis – who is offered a job by a local mobster – played by Walter Matthau. Danny is a great success – but things go badly wrong when he becomes romantically involved with the mobster's girlfriend. With top production values and respected director Michael Curtiz, the movie earned Elvis his best reviews so far. The soundtrack for *King Creole* included two of Elvis's legendary songs, 'Hard Headed Woman' and 'Trouble'.

Leaving Memphis

Opposite: As the bus leaves Memphis for Fort Chaffee, Arkansas, a sad group of women watch Elvis go – including his current girlfriend, Anita Wood (center). Press from around the world are on hand to record the entire proceedings and they follow the bus as it sets off.

Many of Elvis's loyal female fans turn up to tell him they will not forget him while he is away, and Elvis happily chats to them and signs autographs. The press are constantly present with the Army's permission – although when one photographer hides in the barracks at Fort Chaffee to try and get a picture of Elvis sleeping in his bunk, it is decided that things have gone too far and the hapless snapper is thrown out.

Hair today

Elvis runs a comb through his trademark locks, which are due to be shorn the following day. When he is issued with $7 in partial pay, the reporters ask what he will do with all the money, and Elvis jokingly replies that he plans to start a loan company.

Gone tomorrow

There were 55 reporters and photographers on hand to record the famous haircut. Elvis held up some of the hair for the press, and joked, 'Hair today, gone tomorrow!'

Shot three times

The new-look Elvis faces the cameras. All the publicity surrounding the event got Elvis so flustered that he forgot to pay the barber his 65 cent fee, and had to be called back – much to his embarrassment.

Opposite: The Army shoots Elvis three times, when he gets his jabs for typhoid, tetanus and Asian flu. As well as medical tests and a haircut, he also had to do five hours of aptitude tests and sit through a two-hour lecture on a private's rights and privileges.

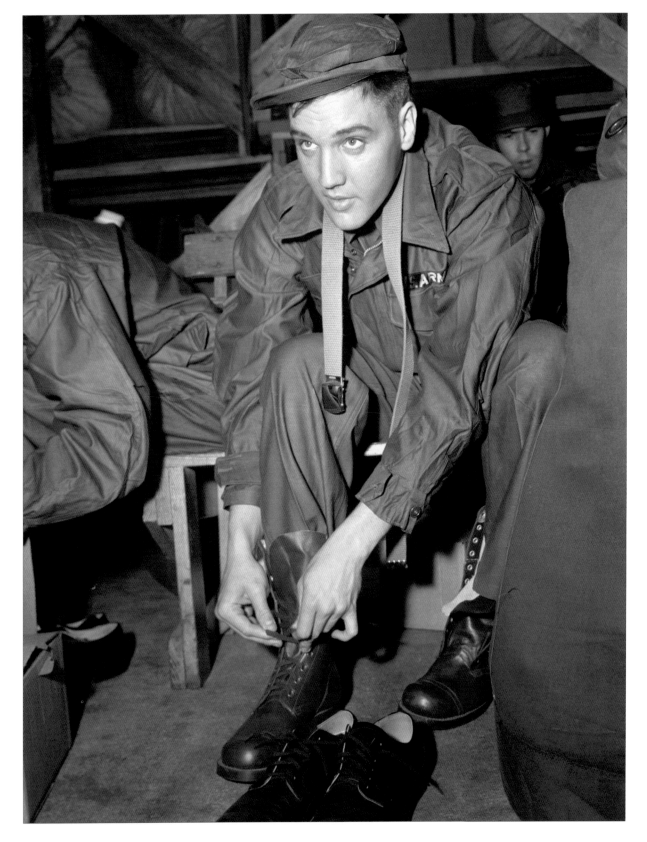

Fitted out for service

Opposite: Elvis tries on some snappy footwear and displays the latest design in Army fatigues. He dealt with all the press attention with great patience and good humor, only refusing to sign autographs while he was 'in ranks'.

It was soon announced that Elvis was to be assigned to the 2nd Armored Division at Fort Hood just outside Killeen in Texas, to do his basic training and advanced tank instruction. The 2nd Armored was General George Patton's famous 'Hell on Wheels' outfit. Six of the other Memphis draftees were also to be sent to Fort Hood, where basic training would last for eight weeks. There was no sign of the press attention letting up, so the Army was beginning to re-think its policy of full access.

A medal for sharpshooting…

Vernon Presley admires his son's medals. Elvis had earned his marksman medal with a carbine and his sharpshooter medal with a pistol and was now acting assistant squad leader. He told reporters that he had gradually been accepted by the others – he had never asked for anything and just did the same as everyone else.

Sneaking a preview

Left: During his leave, Elvis and his parents attended a sneak preview of *King Creole*, which was held in Memphis.

Below: Elvis was always happy to come down to the gates of Graceland to sign autographs and chat to the fans. When reporters asked him why he was wearing his uniform while on leave, he replied 'I'm kinda proud of it.' He also told them that he had adjusted to Army hours and was now having trouble staying awake after midnight.

Just visiting

Anita Wood smiles for photographers as she boards a plane to Texas. She was off to visit Elvis now he had returned to base. She stayed with Sergeant Norwood and his wife at their home on the base.

August 1958: Elvis mourns his mother

Below: In August 1958, Gladys Presley was admitted to
hospital. The diagnosis was uncertain, but her illness was
serious enough for Elvis to be given compassionate leave.
He went straight to the hospital, where Vernon was already
staying – sleeping in a folding cot next to the hospital bed.
His visit seemed to cheer Gladys up and for a time the
doctors thought she might recover.

Opposite: In the early hours of Thursday morning
Gladys died of a heart attack. When reporters turned
up at Graceland later in the day, they found Vernon
and Elvis sitting on the steps of the house. Elvis,
sobbing uncontrollably, told them that his mother
was all they had lived for and that she had always
been his 'best girl'.

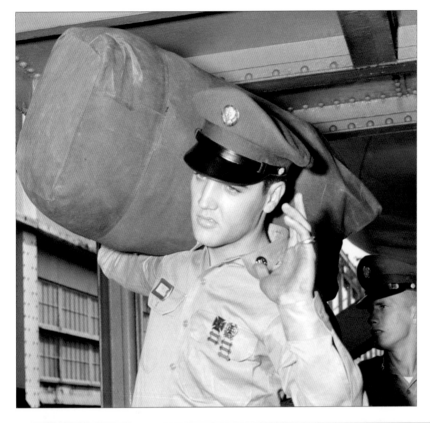

September '58: Off over the sea

Just over a week after the funeral Elvis had to return to Fort Hood to complete his basic training and a month later his unit left for Germany. Since 125 newsmen had arrived in New York to see him off, a press conference and photo opportunity were organized before he boarded the ship. His kit had already been loaded, so a borrowed duffel bag was quickly provided for the pictures.

Below: Although Elvis had never been in Europe, he already had fans there. At least 500 German teenagers arrived to welcome him when the ship docked at Bremerhaven. From the docks the soldiers caught a train to the base at Friedberg, near Frankfurt. Elvis waved to fans and to waiting newsmen as the train left the station.

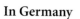

In Germany

Elvis poses in his dress uniform in Germany. At first he was hounded by photographers and bothered constantly by other soldiers looking for autographs, but the press were soon banned from the base and the other soldiers got used to his presence, so things settled down into a routine.

Margit dates her 'very nice boy'

Elvis holding hands with Margit Buergin, a young typist with an electrical supply company in Frankfurt. She had waited outside his hotel to get his autograph and photographers had called for them to kiss. Elvis happily obliged, and he dated Margit several times afterwards. She was only sixteen, but looked older, and still lived with her mother. She told the press that she thought Elvis was 'a very nice boy' and that she liked him very much.

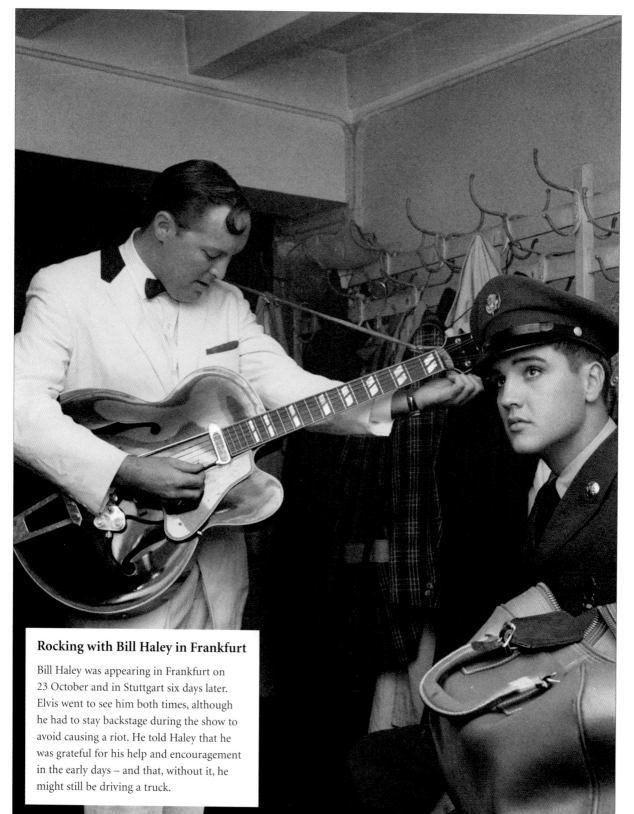

Rocking with Bill Haley in Frankfurt

Bill Haley was appearing in Frankfurt on 23 October and in Stuttgart six days later. Elvis went to see him both times, although he had to stay backstage during the show to avoid causing a riot. He told Haley that he was grateful for his help and encouragement in the early days – and that, without it, he might still be driving a truck.

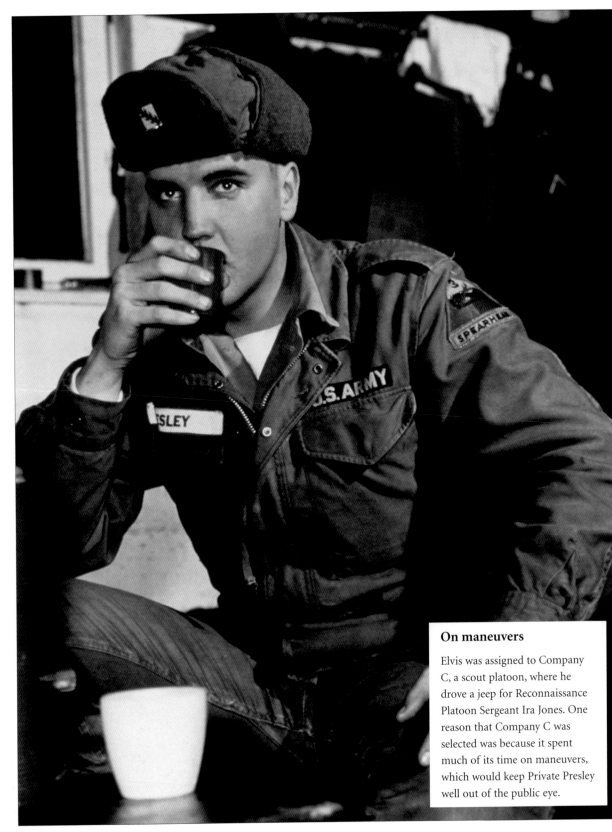

On maneuvers

Elvis was assigned to Company
C, a scout platoon, where he
drove a jeep for Reconnaissance
Platoon Sergeant Ira Jones. One
reason that Company C was
selected was because it spent
much of its time on maneuvers,
which would keep Private Presley
well out of the public eye.

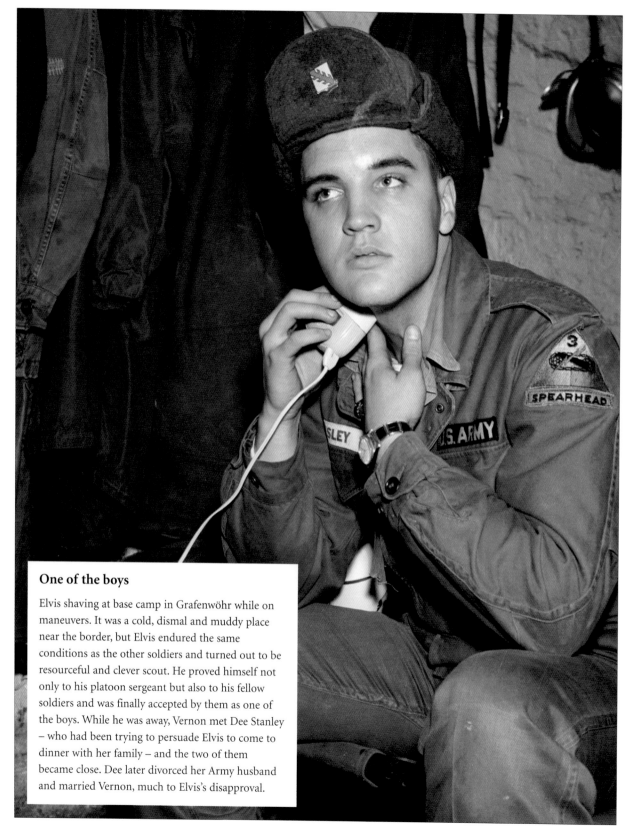

One of the boys

Elvis shaving at base camp in Grafenwöhr while on
maneuvers. It was a cold, dismal and muddy place
near the border, but Elvis endured the same
conditions as the other soldiers and turned out to be
resourceful and clever scout. He proved himself not
only to his platoon sergeant but also to his fellow
soldiers and was finally accepted by them as one of
the boys. While he was away, Vernon met Dee Stanley
– who had been trying to persuade Elvis to come to
dinner with her family – and the two of them
became close. Dee later divorced her Army husband
and married Vernon, much to Elvis's disapproval.

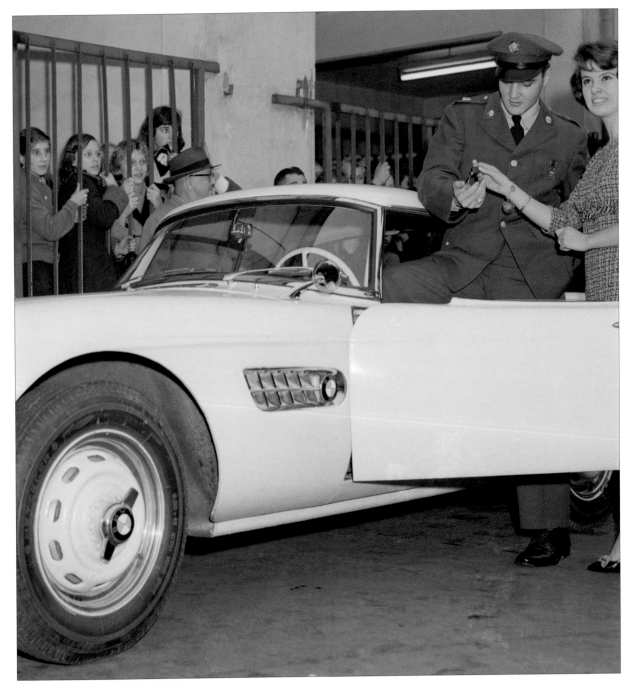

The day after Elvis returned from maneuvers, he took possession of a
second-hand white BMW 507 sports car that had previously been used
by German racer Hans Stuck for demonstrations. At a photo call, the
keys were handed over by a pretty model. He had also bought an old
Cadillac for his father to use and a Volkswagen Beetle for the boys. The
first Christmas in Germany was sad for everyone, not only because they
were away from home but because it was the first without Gladys.

Opposite: Elvis demonstrates the equipment
in his jeep to four-year-old Michael Jones,
the son of his platoon sergeant, at an Open
House held at the 3rd Armored Division
headquarters in Friedberg in April 1959.

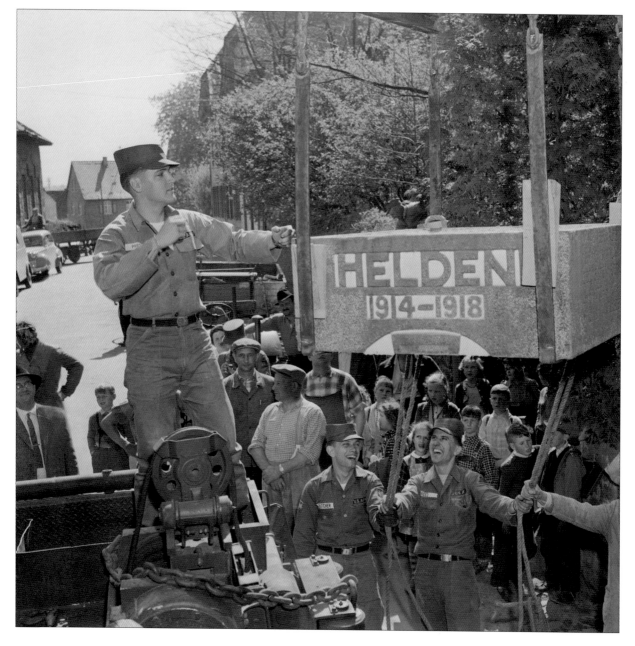

All teamwork but no touring

During the time he was in Germany, Elvis never once appeared on stage or sang for a proper audience. He had been instructed not to do so by Colonel Tom Parker – partly so that he would not be treated differently, but also partly because the Colonel did not see why the Army should get for free what everyone else was prepared to pay a fortune for. Back home, the Colonel was using Elvis's absence and the shortage of material to up the ante in all his negotiations with RCA and the Hollywood studios.

Above: When a World War I memorial in a German village had to be moved to a new location, the US Army stepped in to help. Private Presley directed operations as the sections were lifted by crane. Later he told the press that he thought he and the other soldiers had worked pretty well as a team.

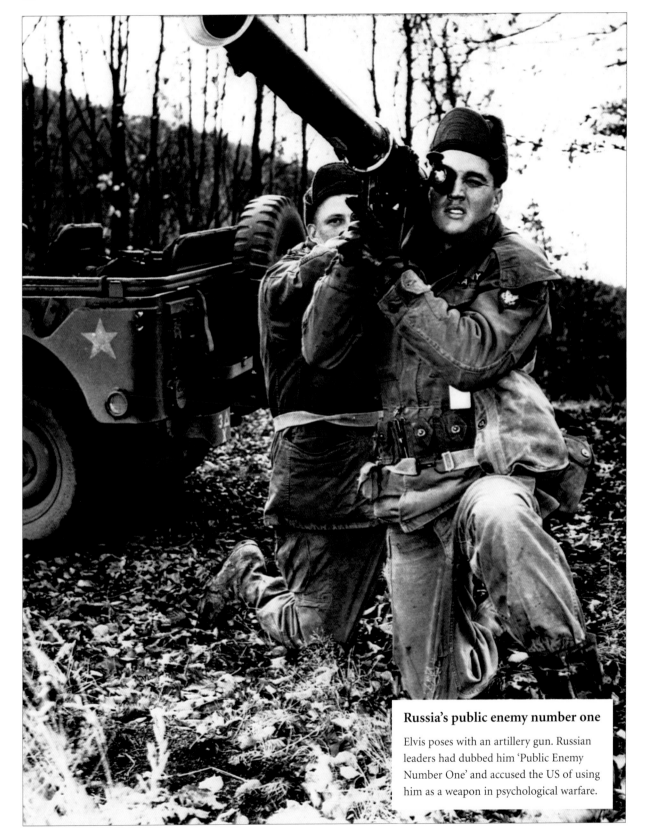

Russia's public enemy number one

Elvis poses with an artillery gun. Russian
leaders had dubbed him 'Public Enemy
Number One' and accused the US of using
him as a weapon in psychological warfare.

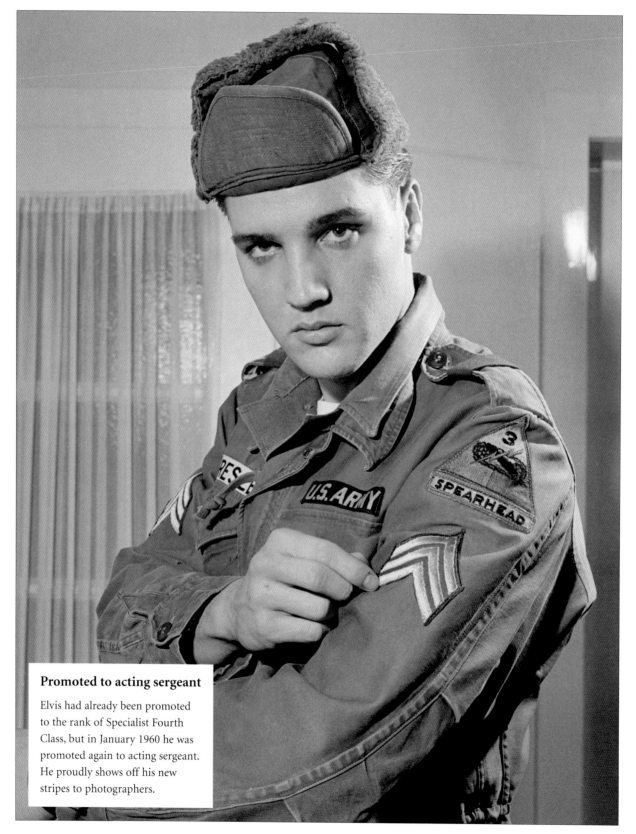

Promoted to acting sergeant

Elvis had already been promoted
to the rank of Specialist Fourth
Class, but in January 1960 he was
promoted again to acting sergeant.
He proudly shows off his new
stripes to photographers.

Sergeant Presley is no richer

Opposite: The advancement in rank carried no increase in pay, but since Elvis was considerably richer than most soldiers, this did not concern him!

Below: While he was in Germany, Elvis did not live on base with the other soldiers. His family and a couple of the Memphis Mafia were there with him and at first they stayed in a series of hotels. After a shaving cream fight and an incident when a small fire set off all the alarms, they were asked to move out, so Elvis rented a house at Goethestrasse 14. Here his grandmother was able to cook the kind of food he liked – and Elvis was often able to slip back home for lunch.

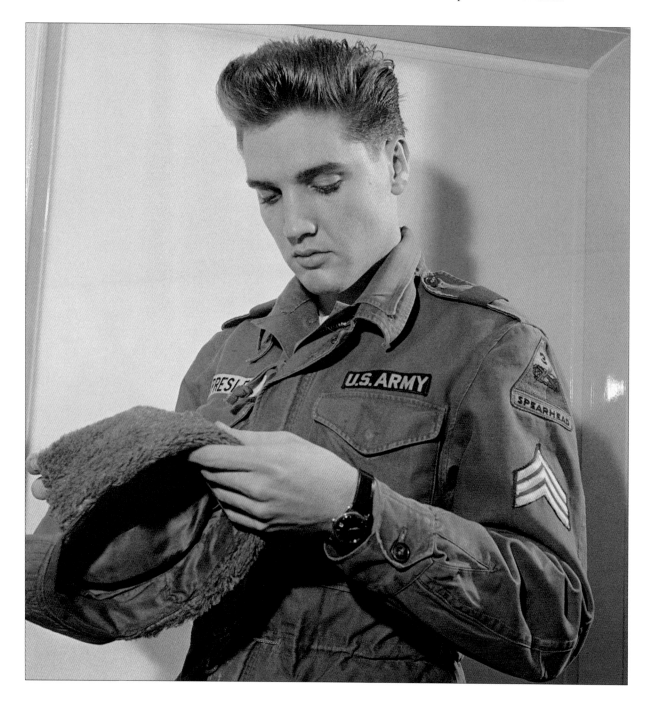

Back in the field…

Sergeant Elvis Presley warms his hands by
the camp fire. By this time he had been made
up to full rank and his platoon were back out
on maneuvers at Grafenwöhr – and it was
the middle of winter and bitterly cold. Elvis
was looking forward to his discharge – he
had only a couple more months to go.

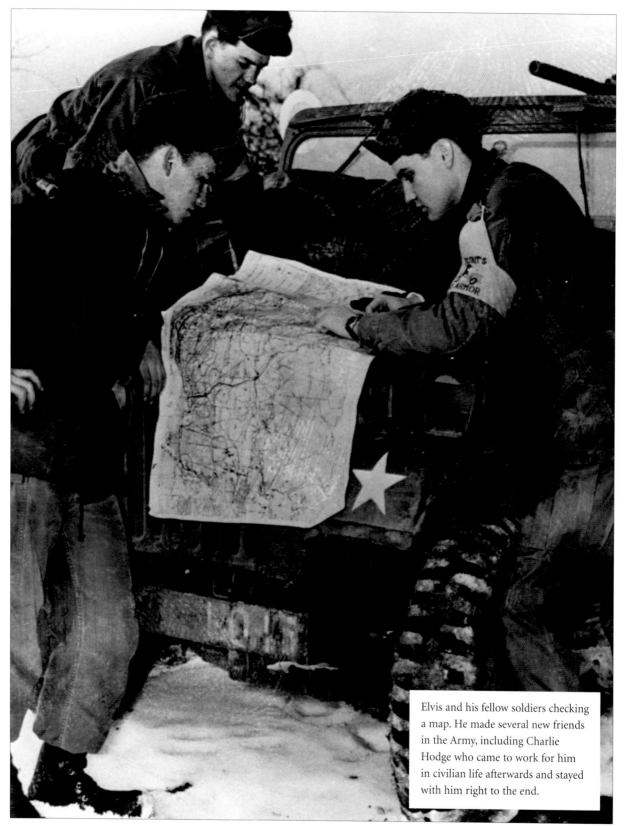

Elvis and his fellow soldiers checking a map. He made several new friends in the Army, including Charlie Hodge who came to work for him in civilian life afterwards and stayed with him right to the end.

Colonel Parker holds the fort

The whole time Elvis was away, the Colonel kept his name in the public eye by judicious release of the material available. He also made sure the fan clubs were kept informed and sent out over four thousand telegrams and messages to fellow performers on his and Elvis's behalf. At a time when the industry was in a slump, he managed to keep Elvis on top. Here he gets a little extra publicity by presenting a whole ham to a state governor.

Elvis in Paris

Left: The Army was not all mud and guns – here Elvis enjoys a few days R&R in Paris, where he stayed in the Prince de Galles in Avenue Georges V with Lamar Fike, Charlie Hodge and Rex Mansfield. They visited famous nightclubs such as the Moulin Rouge and the Folies Bergère and once took the entire chorus line of Bluebell girls from the Lido back to their hotel. They had so much fun in Paris that Elvis decided to stay one more night, paying for a limousine to drive them all back to Friedberg the following day.

Below: Then it was back to active service again.

Back to civilian life

Above: Donning his fatigues for the last time, Elvis studies himself in the mirror. He had survived two years in the Army and was now about to go home again. He told most of his Army buddies that he was looking forward to making more movies and hoped to do more serious roles – but to closer friends he confided that he was afraid the fans would have forgotten him.

Left: Elvis faces journalists at a last press conference in Germany in March 1960, before leaving for the US. He told newsmen that he had learned a lot from the Army and his commanding officer, General Richard J Brown, gave him a special certificate of merit for 'cheerfulness and drive and continually outstanding leadership ability'.

Goodbye

Priscilla Beaulieu waves goodbye as Elvis departs from Rhine-Main air base. When reporters asked about her, Elvis had said she was a 'nice girl' whom he had seen several times. Although he had promised to keep in touch, she was certain that she would never see him again.

A snowy homecoming

Sergeant Elvis Presley carries his bags through the snow, after arriving in New Jersey from Germany in March 1960. He was transferred to Fort Dix, where he stayed for 48 hours until he was officially discharged.

Opposite top: Back in Germany Priscilla is pictured with her photograph of Elvis as she writes him a letter. All the papers referred to her as his 16-year-old girlfriend, but at the time she was still only 14 – although she was very mature for her age. Her family had insisted on meeting Elvis before they would let her see him regularly, but were won over by his charm and sincerity.

Opposite bottom: The press were on hand again to record every step of the discharge proceedings. Here Elvis boards a bus at Fort Dix that will take him from his orientation lecture to the base finance building to collect his final pay.

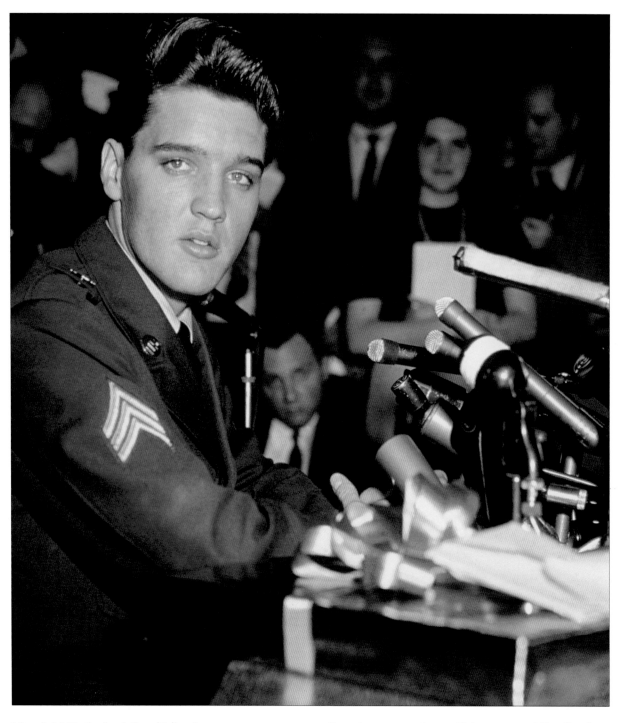

March 1960: Parker's 'boy' is back

Opposite: Colonel Parker looks on as Elvis waves to fans. He had carefully orchestrated all the details of the homecoming, making sure that the fans were around to give Elvis the kind of welcome he deserved – and prove once and for all that Elvis was still on top.

Above: At a press conference, Elvis wore a specially-tailored formal dress uniform – but the tailor had made a mistake with the stripes. The extra rocker on the shoulder designated a rank of staff sergeant, but Elvis had only made sergeant. Some reporters accepted it was a mistake – the more cynical blamed the Colonel for trying to build up the reputation of 'his boy'.

Back to work – and play

Above: Lucky fan Barbara Ann Murray of Roselle Park, New Jersey, gets to sit on Elvis's lap and receives a kiss.

Right: Actress Tina Louise, who went on to become the star of *Gilligan's Island*, interviews Elvis for the cameras.

Opposite: With his hair already beginning to grow out of the regulation Army haircut, Elvis was beginning to look more like the King of Rock 'n' Roll again. He told reporters that he planned to rest at home – although in fact he had a busy schedule. He not only had a recording session planned, but also an appearance on the Frank Sinatra Show and was soon to start shooting on a new movie. Instead he told the newsmen about his newfound interest in karate, which he had been studying in Germany.

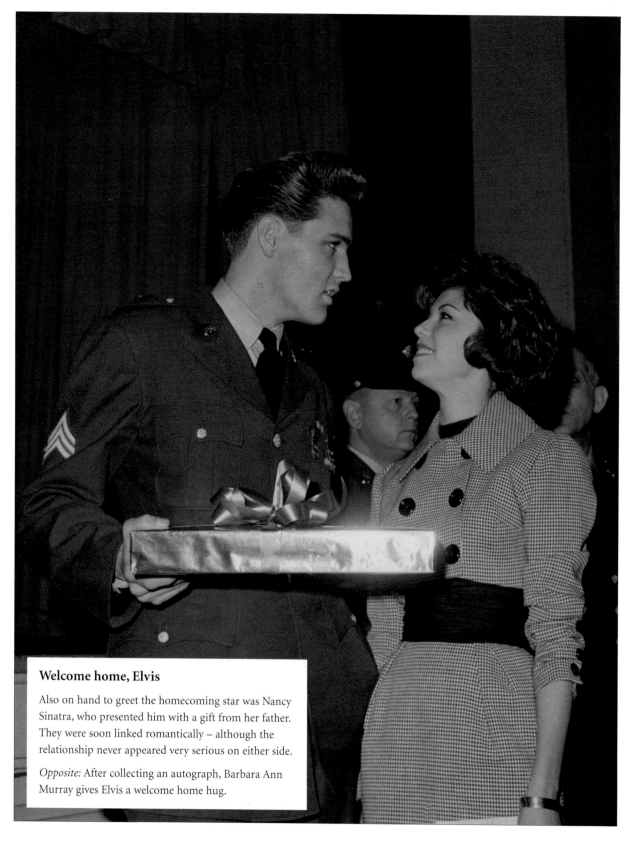

Welcome home, Elvis

Also on hand to greet the homecoming star was Nancy Sinatra, who presented him with a gift from her father. They were soon linked romantically – although the relationship never appeared very serious on either side.

Opposite: After collecting an autograph, Barbara Ann Murray gives Elvis a welcome home hug.

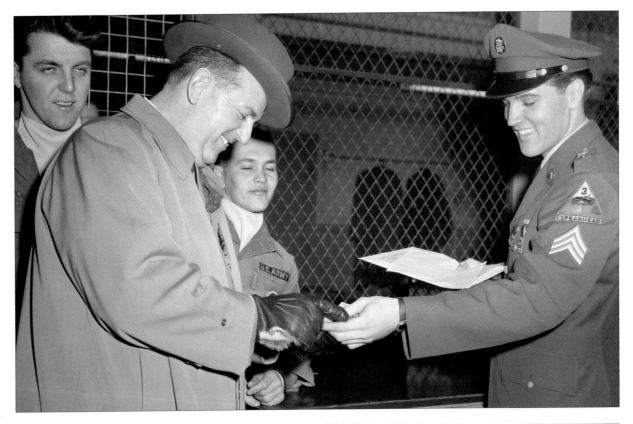

Priscilla: the girl he left behind

Priscilla consoles herself by playing Elvis records back in Germany. She was delighted when he did keep his promise to stay in touch, and soon he was making plans to bring her over to America.

Above: The Colonel reminds Elvis not to forget his commission – and Elvis hands him the entire $109.54.

A duet with Frank

Elvis's appearance on the *Frank Sinatra Show* indicated a change of direction. Perfectly dressed and incredibly elegant in a tuxedo, he sang two songs with professional aplomb, and then did a duet with Sinatra himself. Although some fans mourned the passing of the hell-raising Elvis, most agreed that he had matured and loved the new style.

Elvis, we still love you!

On his train journey down to Miami to record the Sinatra show, almost the entire route was lined with fans and press. Of course the Colonel had taken the trouble to let everyone know Elvis was coming, but it was still an amazing turn out for a singer who had not appeared in concert or recorded any fresh material for nearly two years.

Are You Lonesome Tonight?

As well as appearing with Frank Sinatra, Elvis recorded some classic songs including 'Are You Lonesome Tonight?' and 'It's Now or Never' in the spring of 1960. 'It's Now or Never' went on to sell nine million copies. The LP 'Elvis is Back' was also released and stayed in the *Billboard* chart for 56 weeks. The fans soon resumed their old habits, and Elvis was almost besieged wherever he went.

GI Blues

In May 1960, Elvis began filming *GI Blues*, a musical comedy in which he played a singer serving in the Army. The story borrowed heavily from recent events in Elvis's own life – his character is not only stationed in Germany, he is also in a tank division. The movie was aimed at a general market rather than teenagers and Elvis appears more mature and responsible.

Made in Hollywood

Elvis and Juliet Prowse in a scene from *GI Blues*.
All the scenes featuring Elvis were shot in
Hollywood, with the location footage in
Germany done at a different time.

GI Blues:
a tremendous success

Although longer since he left the Army, Elvis's hair was never again worn in the duck-tail style he had before. *GI Blues* was tremendously successful at the box office, ranking 14th in box office receipts. Critics approved of his new image – but Elvis worried that the musical numbers did not fit into the plot well and the songs were not as good as in some of his previous movies. Despite his fears, the soundtrack album stayed in the charts longer than many of his others and soon reached No.1.

Co-starring Juliet Prowse

Juliet Prowse watches Elvis try the double bass. As well as Juliet, the movie also starred Sigrid Maier, Leticia Roman, Robert Ivers and James Douglas. It was the last movie in the original three-picture contract with Hal Wallis, but the Colonel soon began to negotiate another, similar deal.

Opposite: Co-star Juliet Prowse was the girlfriend of Frank Sinatra – who was not amused when rumors of an affair with Elvis reached him.

Visited by royalty

While filming was in progress, a stream of important visitors came to see Elvis on set. In just one day he welcomed the King and Queen of Thailand, the wife and daughter of the Brazilian president, and three Scandinavian princesses (seen above) – not to mention Pat Boone, Minnie Pearl and Ernie Ford. The Colonel made sure that everyone knew that he was responsible for the royals – he was tirelessly dedicated to promoting anything that involved 'his boy'.

Opposite: A handsome and relaxed Elvis poses in his costume for *GI Blues.*

Elvis takes a gamble

Elvis with Bobby Darin who was appearing at the Hotel Saharah at Las Vegas. Elvis was in Las Vegas on a short vacation, after filming on *GI Blues* was finished. During the weekend, he lost $10,000 at the crap tables.

Opposite: When *GI Blues* was shown in Mexico City it caused a riot – and the Mexican government promptly banned all Elvis movies.

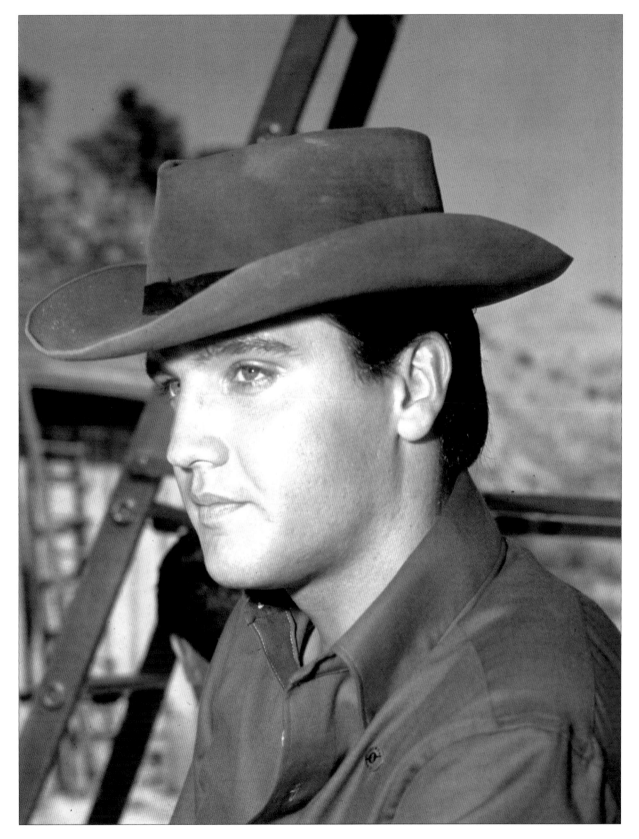

August 1960: Elvis gets serious in *Flaming Star*

In his next movie, *Flaming Star*, Elvis plays Pacer Burton, the son of a white settler and a Kiowa Indian woman, played by Dolores Del Rio. An uprising by the Indians forces Pacer to chose sides – and the storyline also covers the prejudice he encounters as a half-caste. With a respected director, Don Siegal, and a cast of notable actors, *Flaming Star* was the serious movie that Elvis had been wanting to make for some time. Although a version with four songs was also shot, the final release only had two – which greatly disappointed the fans.

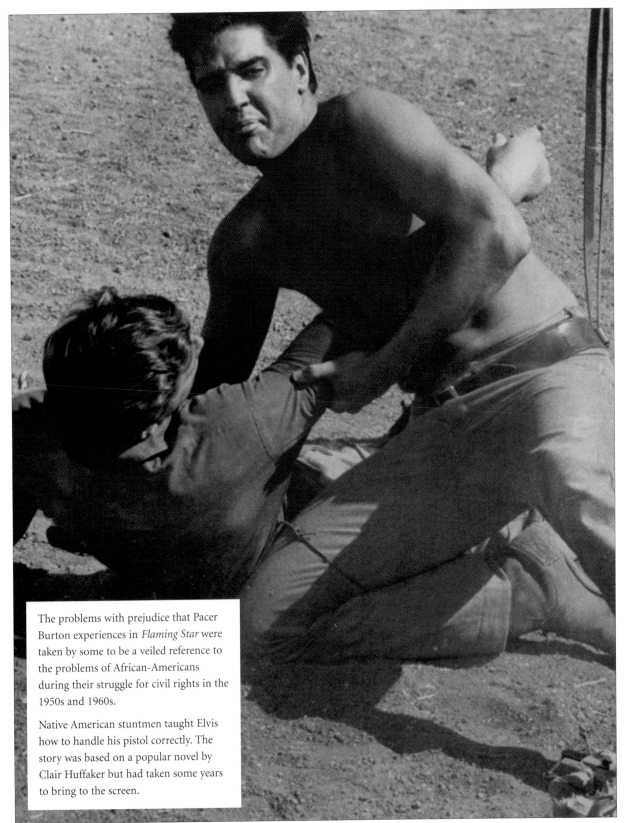

The problems with prejudice that Pacer Burton experiences in *Flaming Star* were taken by some to be a veiled reference to the problems of African-Americans during their struggle for civil rights in the 1950s and 1960s.

Native American stuntmen taught Elvis how to handle his pistol correctly. The story was based on a popular novel by Clair Huffaker but had taken some years to bring to the screen.

Elvis takes a break

Above: Elvis protects Dolores Del Rio as the two of them escape from pursuers. Although *Flaming Star* was a critical success, it did not do as well at the box office as many of Elvis's other movies.

Left: Elvis with Barbara Eden, who played his romantic interest in *Flaming Star*. She later went on to star in the television series *I Dream of Jeannie*.

Opposite: Although Elvis made it through all the rough and tumble of filming without accident, he broke his finger while playing touch football between takes.

Christmas at Graceland 1960

Elvis pictured outside Graceland with his Rolls Royce, just before Christmas 1960.

Opposite top: Chief Wah-Nee-Ota inducts Elvis into the Los Angeles Indian Tribal Council in recognition of his role as a half-caste in *Flaming Star.*

Opposite bottom: Elvis with the Jordanaires recording a song for the soundtrack of one of his movies.

Chapter Four
Are You Lonesome Tonight?

A thoughtful Elvis strums his guitar in a still from the 1961 movie, *Wild in the Country*.

During 1961 Elvis performed live only three times – two concerts at the Ellis Auditorium in Memphis and a charity event for the USS *Arizona* at Bloch Arena at Pearl Harbor, Hawaii. The live appearances had become a danger to all concerned – he had to arrive and leave in the greatest secrecy as the fans behaved so wildly in their attempts to reach him that there was a real risk that someone would soon get hurt. Elvis was also now concentrating on his film career, and since he went on to make three pictures a year for most of the rest of the 1960s there was little time left for concert tours.

The overall quality of Elvis's movies has sometimes been criticised, particularly since at the beginning of his film career several of his directors and fellow actors thought he was capable of even greater things. However, many of his movies were not only highly successful at the box office but were also well received by movie critics. In common with many other musical and comedy stars, almost all his movies were specifically written as a vehicle for their leading man – feel-good stories with lots of songs worked into the script. Elvis himself knew that he could also do darker and more complex roles, given the chance – he said several times in interviews that he wanted to become a serious actor and do dramatic parts. Some people blamed the Colonel for Elvis's failure to widen the range of roles he played, feeling that the desire to make ever more money made the Colonel short-sighted with regard to wider issues. His tireless negotiating for higher fees was certainly a factor in encouraging the studios to play safe and go for the tried and tested to protect their investment. *Flaming Star* and *Wild in the Country* had taken a different line and moved away from singing but they did less well at the box office. On the other hand, *Blue Hawaii*, a lightweight musical comedy built round an exotic location, was a massive hit. Several of the later films were therefore made to a similar formula, but unfortunately some of them suffered from short schedules and tight budgets. Elvis knew that they were not all that he wanted to do, that he had other ambitions to fulfil, but no one could deny that they were making money. Although he was offered some interesting and controversial roles, the Colonel turned them down, both because they did not fit the formula he had established and because they would not have been so lucrative.

Meanwhile, Elvis's personal life was as complicated as ever. At the beginning of the 1960s he was still dating Anita, but seeing other girls whenever she was not around – the Memphis Mafia were always there to cover for him. He had also remained in touch with Priscilla in Germany, and in March 1962 he began to talk to her parents about the possibility of her coming over to America. Understandably they were not sure about the idea, but he arranged for her to stay 'officially' with friends. Priscilla was still only 17, and Elvis himself was conscious of the potential problems if the press found out he was seeing such a young girl. Priscilla finally arrived in Los Angeles and after a few days they left to see Las Vegas, but all too soon she had to return. Despite all their precautions, Anita knew what was happening and decided it was time to move on.

Priscilla returned a few months later, to spend Christmas with Elvis at Graceland. Again the time seemed too short, so Elvis came up with the idea that she should stay in America and finish her schooling at a local Catholic school. Her parents refused to consider it at first, but eventually they gave in. Priscilla moved in with Dee and Vernon and was enrolled in the Immaculate Conception High School, but since Elvis was away in Hollywood working on yet another film, she soon moved into Graceland. When he was at home they did everything together and he began to mould her into his perfect woman,

Tuesday Weld played an uneducated country girl with an illegitimate child in *Wild in the Country*. Throughout filming, there were rumors in the press that the two of them planned to get married. They did become close and stayed friends for many years afterwards.

but she found it difficult to get used to having so many people around. In Germany only a couple of his cronies had been with him, so they had often had time alone together. Now there always seemed to be a crowd of people and she often felt out of place amongst the Memphis Mafia and their older wives and girlfriends.

Things soon became even more complicated. The co-star of Elvis's next movie was Ann-Margret, and she and Elvis quickly realized that they were kindred spirits. Unlike Priscilla, who was shy and terrified of putting a foot wrong with Elvis's entourage, Ann-Margret was full of energy and mischief and soon came to be regarded as one of the boys. Several people commented that they had never seen Elvis so happy, and word began to leak into the papers that she and Elvis were an item. It came to a head when Ann-Margret went to London for the royal première of her previous movie and the British press reported that she had talked of marrying Elvis. The US papers quickly picked up the story; Priscilla was furious and upset – and so was Elvis. He assured the press that if he planned to marry they would hear about it from him, and to Priscilla he denied everything and told her she was the only woman for him. Ann-Margret later refuted the claims that she had said anything but, although she and Elvis remained in contact and continued to see each other in secret, from then on they began to drift apart.

By 1964 The Beatles had hit America and were blasting through the charts, but Elvis had not had a major hit since 'Return to Sender' in 1962. He had somehow lost his direction and he felt increasingly unhappy, lonely and empty. At this point he met hairdresser Larry Geller, who introduced him to spirituality and the search for self-knowledge. Most of those around him did not share his interest and resented the newcomer, but Elvis became immersed

in his new way of life and spent as much time as possible studying over the next couple of years. Despite this, he was also still relying heavily on amphetamines – as were most members of the Memphis Mafia. It all came to a head when he missed the start of filming on his new picture, *Clambake*, saying he was sick. The Colonel demanded a doctor's certificate and although a local doctor, Dr George Nichopoulos, provided one, the Colonel decided things had gone far enough. Elvis was not focusing on business – and since the movies were currently not making as much money as they had, this was no time for 'his boy' to become unreliable. The Colonel fired some of the entourage and made sure Geller was gradually excluded, after which Elvis soon began to return to his old interests.

There was now also Elvis's forthcoming wedding to prepare for. Priscilla had been living at Graceland for more than three years and both she and her father – and the Colonel – had been dropping heavy hints to Elvis about fulfilling his commitments. They finally became engaged at Christmas 1966, and the wedding was set for 1 May 1967, in Las Vegas. The ceremony itself was private – even the Memphis Mafia and their wives and girlfriends were excluded, although they were invited to the reception. Afterwards the newlyweds went back to Palm Springs and then on to the Flying Circle G in Mississippi, the ranch that Elvis had bought earlier that year. Although several members of the entourage came with them, Priscilla later said it was an idyllic time in which their privacy was respected and she was able to enjoy looking after her new husband herself. At the end of the month they returned to Graceland and had another big reception for those who had missed the first. Within a few weeks, Priscilla realized she was pregnant. At first she was upset, because for the first time she had been feeling a real part of Elvis's life in America and now everything would inevitably change, but Elvis was delighted at the prospect of becoming a father. After Lisa Marie Presley was born on 1 February 1968, Elvis announced that he was the happiest man in the world.

Although his personal life seemed to have settled down, the problems in Elvis's career now came to a head. The fans were less devoted to seeing Elvis in every movie he made, and although a gospel album, *How Great Thou Art*, was selling steadily, his other records were not doing that well. The songs being supplied for movie soundtracks were often so formulaic that even the Colonel was moved to protest. Unfortunately, much of the reason for that went back to the old arrangements he himself had set

up for writers requiring them to forgo part of their royalty before Elvis would record their song. Understandably, the best material was now no longer offered to him.

A change of direction was clearly needed and Elvis was ready to make it. The Colonel had arranged for him to appear in a TV special, which was to be broadcast just before Christmas 1968. It was to be recorded before a live audience – the first time Elvis had sung on stage for seven years. The Colonel wanted 'his boy' to sing a straightforward selection of Christmas songs, but NBC producer Bob Finkel convinced Elvis to go for a radical change of image. Director Steve Binder put together a show that

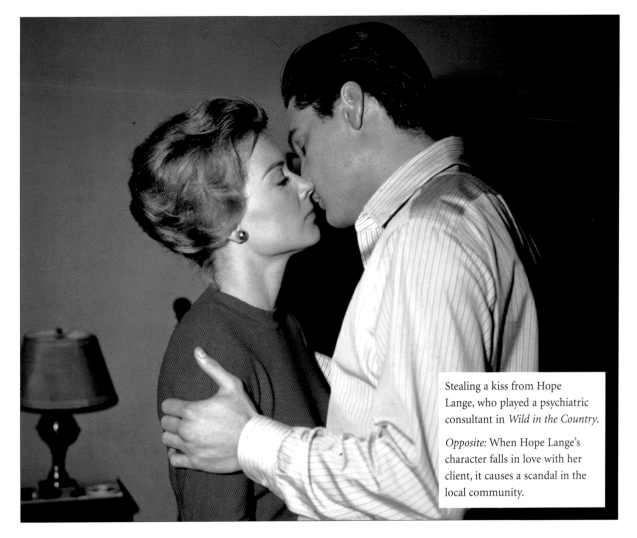

Stealing a kiss from Hope Lange, who played a psychiatric consultant in *Wild in the Country*.

Opposite: When Hope Lange's character falls in love with her client, it causes a scandal in the local community.

featured Elvis in black leather belting out his rock 'n' roll hits, and finished with a brand new song, 'If I Can Dream'. It was a total triumph. Everyone had forgotten what Elvis was capable of and hearing him sing the old hits with an exciting new freshness was a revelation to many.

Elvis himself was now determined to return to touring. From his new position of strength, the Colonel arranged a four-week booking at the brand-new International Hotel that was due to open in Las Vegas that July. It was certainly a gamble: Elvis's only previous appearance in Las Vegas had been a disaster; the room he was being expected to fill had a capacity almost twice those that current major headliners played; and it would all take place in a full glare of publicity. Meanwhile, some changes

had also been made in terms of how the records were recorded. The last few studio sessions in Nashville had been fairly disastrous, with only the minimum usable material laid down. Elvis was persuaded to try American, a small new studio in Memphis that had produced a string of hits under the direction of its principal owner, Chips Moman. The sessions were an unqualified success and Elvis recorded some of his best material to date, with the first single released, 'In the Ghetto', giving him a major hit and another gold record.

The opening night in Las Vegas on 31 July 1969, was the first time Elvis had performed a full concert in public for more than eight years. He was visibly nervous beforehand, but when he came out on stage and launched into his first number, his uninhibited

Fans cluster around a lei-clad Elvis as he
stands in Los Angeles airport before
flying to Hawaii to star in his next movie,
Blue Hawaii. He was also scheduled to
make several benefit appearances during
his three-week stay on the island.

Can't Help Falling in Love

During a scene from *Blue Hawaii*, Elvis sings to a bevy of Hawaiian beauties. A musical comedy, this was one of the most commercially successful of Elvis's movies. 'Can't Help Falling in Love', from the soundtrack of *Blue Hawaii*, was released as a single in October 1961 and went on to become a massive hit that year.

Behind bars again!

In *Blue Hawaii*, Elvis played Chad Gates, the son of a wealthy plantation owner.
Pressured by his parents to give up his easy-going lifestyle to help run the family
business, Chad disappears to the beach to play music with his native Hawaiian friends.

Opposite top: In a scene from the movie, Guy Lee as Ping Pong tries to spray water at
Roland Winters as Fred Gates, Elvis, Angela Lansbury as Sarah Lee Gates and John
Archer as Fred Kelman.

Opposite bottom: The soundtrack of *Blue Hawaii* featured 14 other numbers as well
as 'Can't Help Falling in Love'. The music ranged across several musical styles.
There were extensive shots of the Hawaiian scenery, with shooting at Waikiki Beach,
Hanauma Bay and Ala Moana Park.

Dreading deep water...

Opposite: Angela Lansbury was cast as Elvis's mother – although she was only 35 at the time.

Joan Blackman with Elvis on the beach. During the filming of *Blue Hawaii*, Elvis revealed that he was apprehensive in deep water. Director Norman Taurog gave him the option of doing scenes on the beach instead, but Elvis bravely faced his fear and most of them were shot in or on the ocean, as originally called for in the script.

1962: Return to Sender

Above: In a fit of anger, Elvis slugs Jeremy Slate, who has tried to steal his girl. *Girls! Girls! Girls!* was shot in Hawaii.

Otis Blackwell's 'Return to Sender', which featured in the movie, was released as a single in October 1962.

Laurel Goodwin had the part of Elvis's love interest in *Girls! Girls! Girls!*

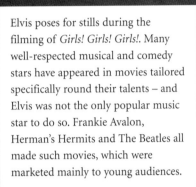

Elvis poses for stills during the
filming of *Girls! Girls! Girls!*. Many
well-respected musical and comedy
stars have appeared in movies tailored
specifically round their talents – and
Elvis was not the only popular music
star to do so. Frankie Avalon,
Herman's Hermits and The Beatles all
made such movies, which were
marketed mainly to young audiences.

Summer of 1962

Elvis and his entourage arrive in Seattle, accompanied by police officers. They had come to the city for location filming for *It Happened at the World's Fair* – the 1962 World's Fair was being held there at the time.

Opposite: Elvis gets a manicure on Seattle's monorail. He and the guys were prone to elaborate jokes to liven up the boredom of filming. One of their favorites was to call for room service after having removed all the furniture from the room – then to have it all back in place by the time the manager arrived.

$9300 wardrobe

The storyline of *Fun in Acapulco* had Elvis as a former trapeze artist, who develops a phobia after his partner is severely injured. He gets a job as a lifeguard in a luxurious Mexican resort instead, and falls in love with the hotel's social director, played by Ursula Andress. Exteriors were shot on location in Mexico, but Elvis stayed on the Paramount lot in Hollywood. *Fun in Acapulco* went on to become the top-grossing movie of 1963.

Opposite: Hitching a ride to the World's Fair. The Colonel always made sure there were plenty of photographers on set, and planted a story about Elvis's new wardrobe that had been supplied for the movie. Hollywood couturier Sy Devore explained that the entire wardrobe cost $9300 – but did not include underwear as Elvis did not wear any.

1963: Viva Las Vegas

Ann-Margret and Elvis
during filming of *Viva Las
Vegas* for MGM in 1963.
Ann-Margret was known
as the 'female Elvis Presley'
because of her sensual
performing style, and
rumors quickly began
circulating that the two
stars were having an affair.
This time the rumors were
true – despite the fact that
Priscilla was already
quietly living at Graceland.

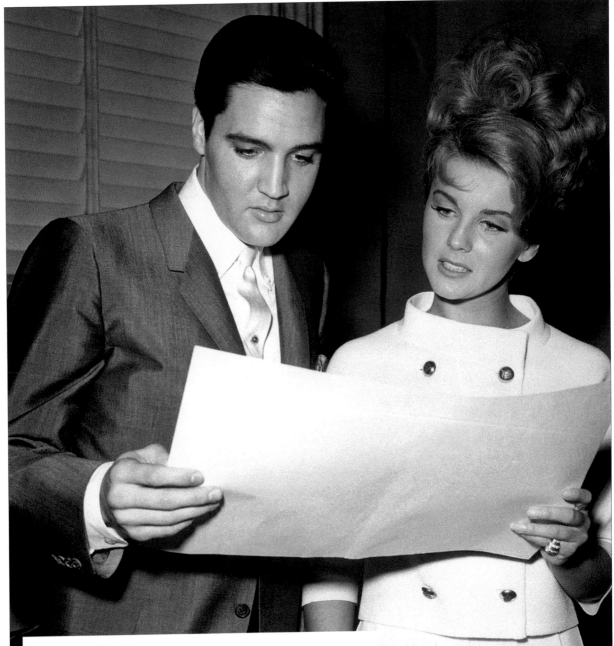

On-screen chemistry…

Elvis and Ann-Margret study one of the songs that they are to sing in *Viva Las Vegas*. Because of the sexual chemistry between the two stars, the musical numbers in the movie vibrate with a sensual passion not found in Elvis's other movies.

Opposite: Elvis and Ann-Margret shared a love of motorcycles – much to the consternation of production staff, since an accident to either of them could have delayed filming for many weeks.

Elvis and Ann-Margret get serious

The affair with Ann-Margret was the most serious that Elvis had with any of his co-stars. However, she was serious about her career and certainly did not want to give it up for marriage at this stage. Elvis also had Priscilla to consider – to get her father's permission to bring her over to the US from Germany, he had apparently promised that they would get married one day.

Just good friends?

Even after their romance cooled, Elvis and Ann-Margret
stayed close friends – right up to the end of his life –
and he always sent flowers to her on opening nights.

Priscilla stays out of the public eye

Elvis enjoys a few nights off in Las Vegas. Priscilla was never seen with him in public during this period – everyone was afraid of what the press would make of the fact that he had such a young girl staying in his home, even though she was well-chaperoned.

Meeting James Brown

A group of Las Vegas showgirls are eager to chat to their celebrity guest.

Opposite: During a break in filming of their respective movies, James Brown drops in on Elvis for a chat. Elvis had long been an admirer of the other singer's work and had wanted to meet him for some time. Elvis was currently filming *Roustabout*, in which he played a carnival hand with a knack for getting into trouble. Barbara Stanwyck was the boss and the two stars initially did not get on. Later they became friends and Elvis said the experience of working with her had inspired him to become a better actor.

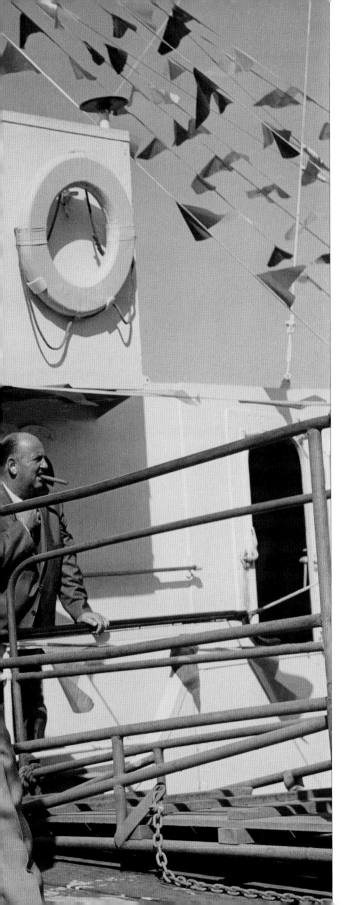

White elephant…

In 1964, it was announced that Elvis had bought the USS *Potomac* for $55,000. The boat had been President Roosevelt's 'floating White House' during the Second World War but had been pensioned off from active service to act as a tourist attraction in Long Beach. The owners had planned to auction it on the 82nd anniversary of Roosevelt's birth and the Colonel decided that Elvis should buy it and present it to the March of Dimes. Unfortunately it was far too expensive to maintain for the March of Dimes to accept, so they turned down the offer. The Coast Guard Unit in Miami also refused to accept it and newspapers began to refer to the *Potomac* as a 'white elephant'. Finally, the St Jude Hospital in Memphis, a research center that investigated serious childhood diseases, decided they would take it. The boat was hurriedly painted to impress the press – but there had only been time to do one side. The charity had been founded by comedian Danny Thomas, and he officially accepted the *Potomac* from Elvis in a dedication ceremony held at Long Beach in February. In the background, the Colonel smokes one of his trademark cigars.

March 1964: Filming begins on *Roustabout*

Barbara Stanwyck and Elvis enjoy a ride on the carousel.
Roustabout was set against the background of a small
American carnival – a life that the Colonel certainly
knew inside out. He had suggested the original idea back
in 1961, and as the script developed he came up with
many pieces of 'carny' business to include in the story.

Elvis does his own stunts

Part of the action for *Roustabout* was filmed on location, at Thousand Oaks just northwest of Los Angeles and at the Hidden Valley Ranch in California. Elvis insisted on doing a fight sequence himself, and was hit on the head. He needed four stitches but, since the script called for him to be ridden off the road on his motorcycle, the genuine injury was used and filming continued.

The Colonel's offer

In the story, the carnival boss discovers Elvis's singing talent and uses him to attract crowds to the show.

Opposite top: As well as Barbara Stanwyck, the movie also co-stared Joan Freeman as the girl who fights Elvis all the way, but who eventually falls in love with him. The Stanwyck part was originally offered to Mae West, but she turned it down.

Opposite bottom: Tickle Me was Elvis's first picture for Allied Artists. His salary of $750,000 was half the budget, and he also had a 50% share of the profits. Allied Artists was in financial trouble and the Colonel offered to let them out of their agreement, but studio head Steve Broidy refused.

Taking on the bad guys

Director Norman Taurog, on his fifth
Presley movie, was asked to try and
bring *Tickle Me* in under budget – both
to help Allied Artists and to ensure the
movie was completed. Since he was a
fast and efficient worker, who got on
well with Elvis, he managed to come in
under what was already a tight costing.

Left: Enjoying a joke with one of his
co-stars on the set of *Tickle Me.*
Away from the cameras, Elvis had
found a much more serious interest.
He had recently met Larry Geller, a
hairdresser who had introduced him to
alternative religion.

Opposite: Elvis tackles the bad guy.
Tickle Me saved Allied Artists from
going under, its gross only coming in
behind that of *55 Days in Peking* and
El Cid in the company's history.
It also made the usual profit for Elvis
and the Colonel.

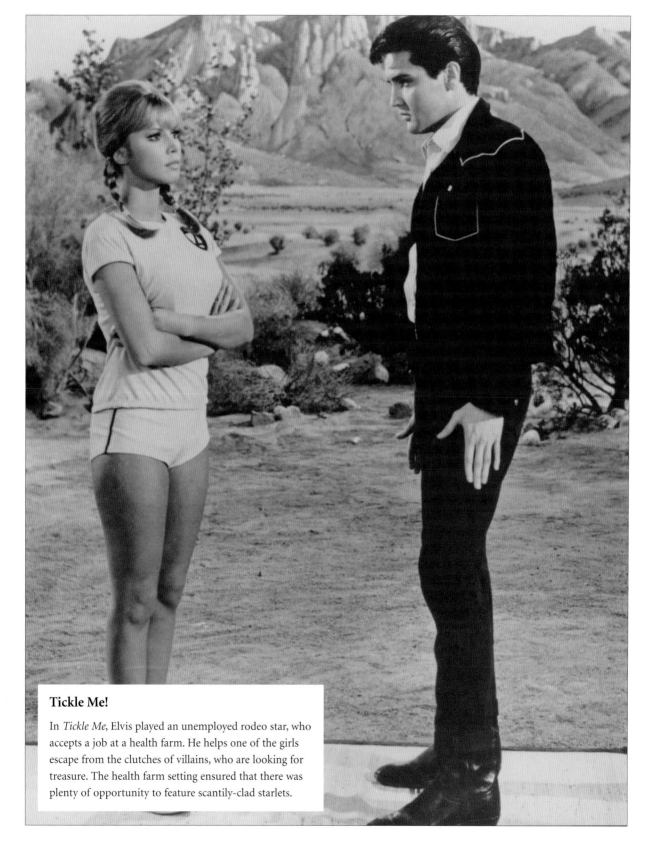

Tickle Me!

In *Tickle Me*, Elvis played an unemployed rodeo star, who accepts a job at a health farm. He helps one of the girls escape from the clutches of villains, who are looking for treasure. The health farm setting ensured that there was plenty of opportunity to feature scantily-clad starlets.

Cutting costs…

One way in which the Colonel maximized profits from *Tickle Me* was to arrange with Allied that the movie soundtrack would only utilize songs already recorded by Elvis – which he guaranteed would not have appeared on a single or EP. In this way they could avoid the costs of recording original soundtrack material, while at the same time still being able to release a soundtrack record.

Many of the songs featured in Elvis's movies are very good – there is 'Return to Sender' from *Girls! Girls! Girls!*, 'Wolf Call' from *Girl Happy* and 'Can't Help Falling in Love' from *Blue Hawaii*. However, since *Tickle Me* did not have an original score, it had to rely on the quality of the songs that the Colonel picked out – although Elvis made the final selection.

1965: Come into the desert…

Harum Scarum was a light-hearted movie, set in the desert, produced by Sam Katzman and directed by Gene Nelson. The costumes were deliberately designed to make Elvis look like a modern Rudolf Valentino.

Above: While Elvis was making *Frankie and Johnnie* for United Artists, he was deeply absorbed by studies of religion, philosophy and the occult. Co-star Donna Douglas was both religious and spiritual, and Elvis spent hours with her discussing the books they had each read. He was rather overweight during filming, but his costumes were cleverly cut to hide it.

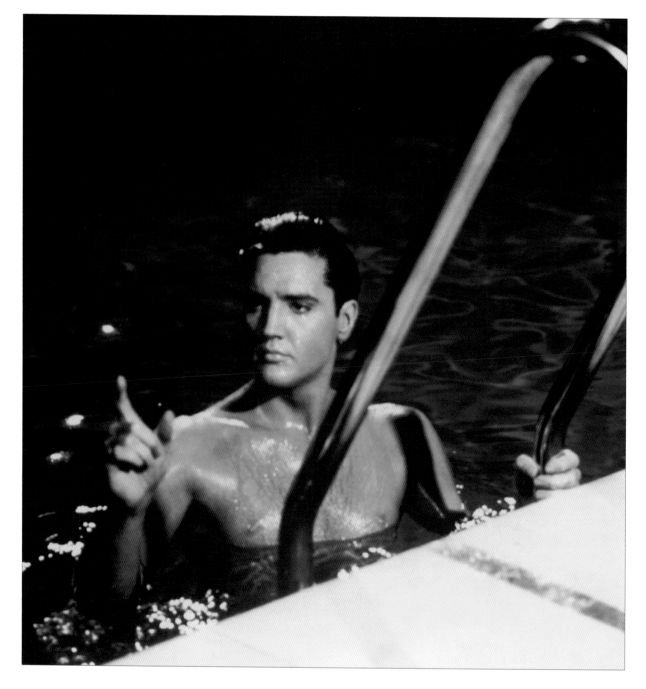

Paradise regained in 1965

In *Paradise, Hawaiian Style*, Elvis played Rick Richards, a helicopter pilot who operates a charter service. He had always enjoyed being in Hawaii before, but this time reporters noted that he seemed rather depressed. Nevertheless, he threw himself into the making of the movie, in which he sang some traditional Hawaiian folk songs.

Elvis had not had a song in the charts for a while, but now 'Crying in the Chapel', which had been recorded some time before and released in April 1965, was a top ten hit.

Action hero

The typical Presley hero was always a man of action, often with an interesting or unusual job – who could also sing. In *Spinout*, a movie for MGM again directed by Norman Taurog, he was a racing driver. The 1929 Duesenberg in which he is supposed to enter the Santa Fe Road Race was a priceless classic car. Despite its glamorous settings and glimpses of a wealthy lifestyle, the movie did not do well at the box office. However, his new single, 'Love Letters', was released in June 1966 and soon went into the top 20.

Elvis in a scene from *Clambake*. He was now filming for much of the year – *Easy Come, Easy Go* had begun shooting just three weeks after *Double Trouble* had finished, although there was then a three-month break before *Clambake* began. The review of *Easy Come, Easy Go* in *Variety* said, 'Anyone who has seen similar movies recognizes the superior quality of Presley's movies: the story makes sense; the songs are better, and better motivated; cast and direction are stronger; production values are first-rate.'

Opposite: Double Trouble was released in April 1967 and – although it did steady business – it did not make the kind of profits that Presley movies were expected to bring in.

1967: Priscilla and Elvis say 'I do'

On 1 May 1967, Elvis and Priscilla Beaulieu are married by Nevada Supreme Court Justice David Zenoff, in a private ceremony held in a suite in the English-Tudor-style Aladdin Hotel in Las Vegas.

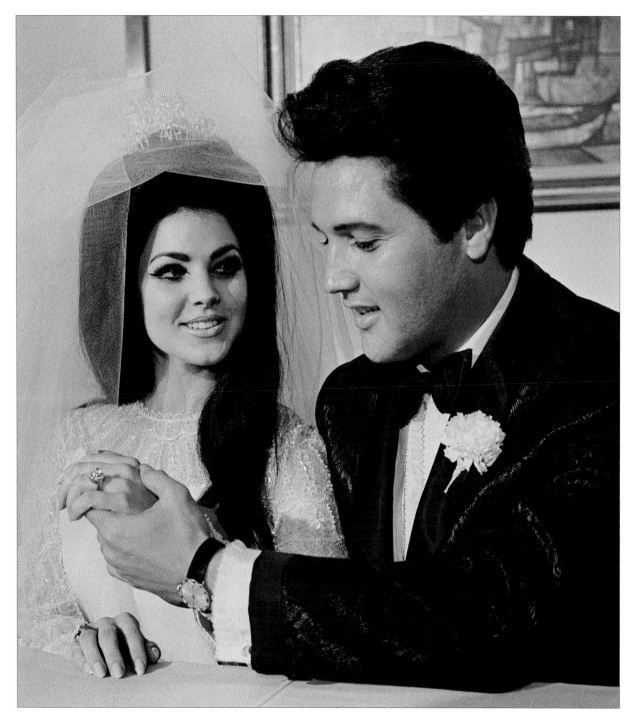

'It was about time' says Elvis

After the eight-minute ceremony was over, a press conference was held in the Aladdin Room of the hotel. Priscilla showed off her three-carat diamond ring and the happy couple kissed for the benefit of photographers. Reporters asked Elvis why he had finally decided to get married, and he replied, 'Well, I guess it was about time.' Priscilla's father told the newsmen that he had known from the beginning that the two of them would get married one day. Priscilla said later that they had both been so nervous before the ceremony that neither of them had slept the previous night.

Celebrating in style

There were over one hundred people at the reception, eating a buffet banquet while a string trio played romantic ballads – including some of the groom's hits. However, most members of the Memphis Mafia had been excluded from the actual ceremony – lack of space in the suite was cited as the reason – and were invited to the reception only. It caused some resentment, and marked the beginning of disaffection in the Mafia ranks.

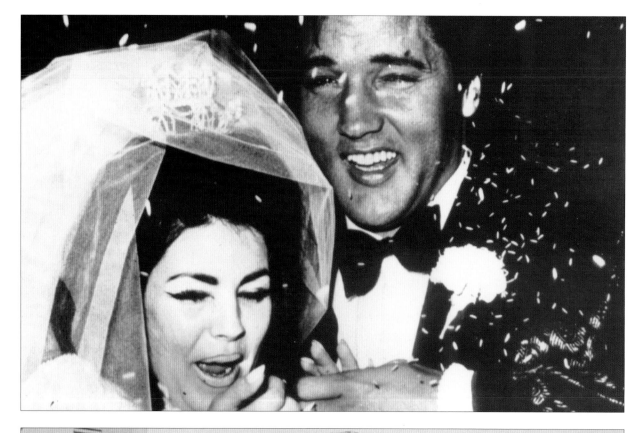

Man and wife

The happy couple returned to Palm Springs after the reception, but three days later left for Memphis and on to the Circle G Ranch. Although most of the Memphis Mafia came with them, living on the ranch without the household staff gave Priscilla a chance to 'play house' and look after her new husband herself. At the end of the month, they held another wedding ceremony at Graceland – a less formal affair that included the entire Graceland staff and all Elvis's uncles, aunts and cousins, as well as his doctor, dentist, painter, horse trainer and electrician.

Love interest

Elvis's co-star and love-interest on *Speedway* was
Nancy Sinatra (opposite), and rumors circulated in
the press that the two of them were having an affair
in real life. They had been linked romantically
several times previously but Elvis just liked to flirt
with any available woman.

Nancy and Elvis

Despite all the rumors, after Lisa Marie was born it was Nancy Sinatra who held a baby shower for Priscilla.

Opposite: When asked by a journalist what kind of part he played in *Speedway*, Elvis answered, 'I'm kinduva singin' millionaire-playboy-race driver, sir.' The journalist went on to ask if Elvis had ever played such a part before, and he replied, 'Only about 25 times, sir.'

Off to the movies again…

In *Speedway*, Elvis played a racing driver for the third time and it was director Norman Taurog's eighth Presley picture. Many of the Memphis Mafia had small roles in the movie – and even Taurog's small granddaughter had a part.

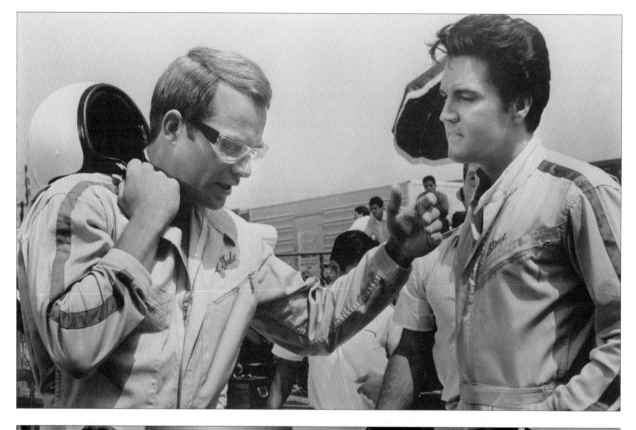

And baby makes three

On 1 February 1968, Priscilla gave birth to a baby girl. Hundreds of fans, nurses, patients and members of the press were waiting to see the new family leave the hospital and drive off in a fleet of Cadillacs and Lincolns.

Welcome Lisa Marie

Priscilla left the Baptist Memorial Hospital in Memphis four days after the birth of Lisa Marie, escorted by Elvis, Vernon and a host of others.

Proud parents

After the birth of his daughter, Elvis told everyone that he was the happiest man in the world. He had often told people over the years that if he had a daughter he would name her Gladys after his mother, but they had finally selected the name Lisa Marie. Both denied there was any significance in either name – although the Colonel's wife was called Marie.

Fun on location in 1967

In *Stay Away, Joe,* Elvis's character was an Indian rodeo rider, Joe Whitecloud, and the storyline pitted Indian ingenuity against government bureaucracy. There were originally only three songs – another was added later.

Opposite top: On the set, Elvis appeared warm and relaxed.

Opposite bottom: Stay Away, Joe had a good cast, with veteran actors Burgess Meredith, Thomas Gomez and Katy Jurado. They all had fun on location – even the Colonel joined in, making a promotional calendar out of a picture of himself taken by the pool with a snarling face and several days' growth of beard.

More mature

A publicity photograph of a more
mature Elvis, taken in 1968.

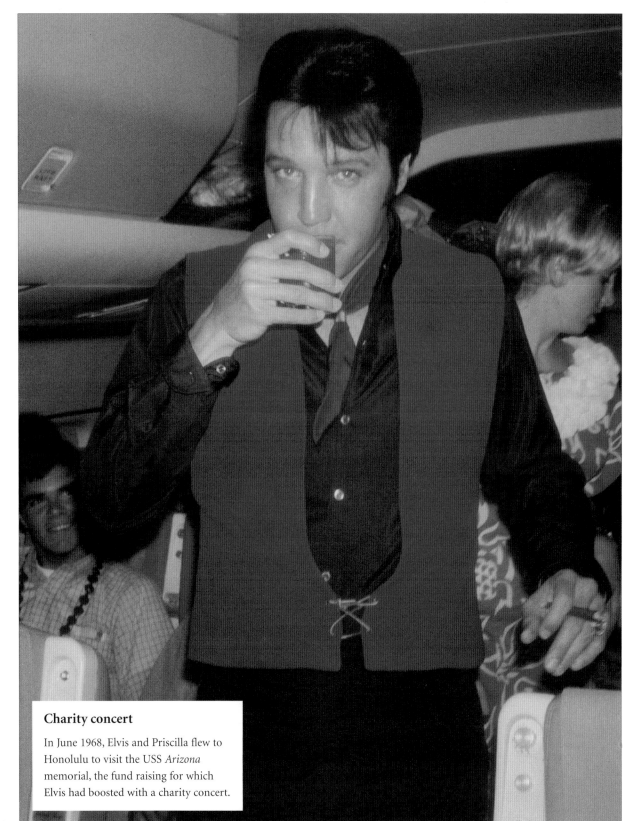

Charity concert

In June 1968, Elvis and Priscilla flew to Honolulu to visit the USS *Arizona* memorial, the fund raising for which Elvis had boosted with a charity concert.

Elvis's change of image

As well as Elvis and Priscilla, the party travelling to Honolulu included several members of the Memphis Mafia and their wives. They were also planning to attend a karate championship at the Honolulu International Center, which was staged by Ed Parker, an old friend of Elvis. On his return from the holiday, Elvis was thinner than he had been for several years and had grown his sideburns longer.

1968: Live a Little, Love a Little

Elvis in *Live a Little, Love a Little*, a comedy movie that was based on a popular novel by Dan Greenburg, *Kiss My Firm but Pliant Lips*. Again the director was Norman Taurog and the screenplay included only four songs.

Elvis tires of filmmaking

In *Live a Little, Love a Little*, Elvis played a successful photographer. By this time he had decided that he wanted to stop making movies but, because of the Colonel's habit of negotiating block contracts, he was contractually obliged to make several more.

Backstage with the 'Welsh Elvis'

A publicity shot from *Live a Little, Love a Little*, with a relaxed and casual Elvis.

Opposite top: Live a Little, Love a Little was released in October 1968, but neither the single nor the movie did very well. It seemed as if Elvis's career had stalled, and something bold was needed to get it going again.

Opposite bottom: Elvis and Priscilla visit Tom Jones backstage at his show in the Flamingo Hotel in Las Vegas. Tom Jones was often compared to an early Elvis in style – and in his appeal to the female fans.

Comeback king

A publicity shot for the forthcoming *Comeback Special* gives little idea of the new-look Elvis that is about to burst onto the TV screen.

Opposite: In his last few movies, Elvis made a break from the kind of things he had done before. *Charro!* was a hard-hitting western, in which the fans were treated to a bearded and rugged Elvis.

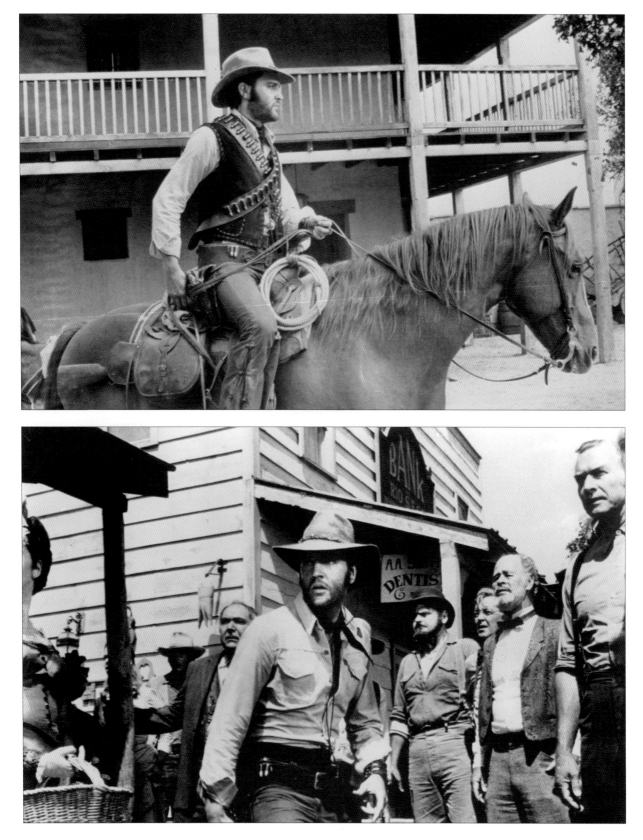

Reformed outlaw

Elvis's character in *Charro!* is a former outlaw, who comes over to the side of law enforcement and then has to stand up to the members of his former gang – who try to frame him for the theft of a valuable cannon that belongs to the Mexican government. Elvis looks unkempt in a dusty outfit and is almost unrecognisable.

The Trouble with Girls in 1968

Above: The Trouble With Girls was set in the 1920s, with Elvis as the manager of a chautauqua – a travelling college that brought culture to rural areas and isolated villages.

Left: Elvis doesn't appear until about one-third of the way into the movie. His main role is to hold together the various sub-plots in the movie.

Christmas 1968: Back to his roots

A leather-clad Elvis shows how it used to be, in the *Comeback Special* aired on NBC at Christmas. The Colonel had originally wanted him merely to sing a few Christmas songs, but NBC producer Steve Binder persuaded him to go back to his roots. He challenged Elvis to walk down the street and see if he was recognized by young people. Elvis was reluctant, since he had not been out without an escort for some years, but he decided to try. When no-one recognized him, he agreed that his career needed a major boost – which meant going against the Colonel's wishes.

Hit album follows *Comeback Special*

The *Comeback Special* featured live segments, pre-filmed concert sequences and casual jamming sessions, and loosely told the story of a young singer finding fame. The critics were ecstatic, praising both his performance and charisma. The show was the highest-rated program that week, and the album that followed was also a hit.

The King is back!

The leather suit that Elvis
wore for the *Comeback Special*
had been specially tailored for
him by Bill Belew, who went
on to design several of the
jumpsuits that Elvis wore in
later years. He looked younger
and more handsome than he
had done for many years.

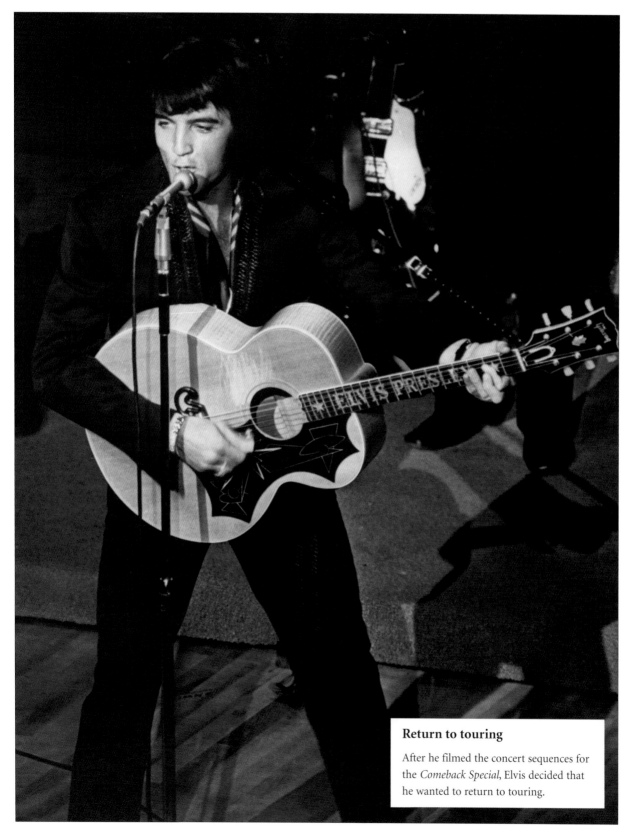

Return to touring

After he filmed the concert sequences for the *Comeback Special*, Elvis decided that he wanted to return to touring.

If I Can Dream

Elvis wore several different outfits during
the various sections of the *Comeback
Special*. At the end, dressed in a white
suit, he sang 'If I Can Dream' which had
been specially written to close the show.
It had reached No 12 in the charts by
January 1969, and went on to become yet
another millionseller.

Jamming with the band

Above: In the informal section of the show, Elvis tried to recreate the atmosphere of the dressing room on the stage. In between jamming with the other musicians, Elvis chatted about events in his career. His words were not scripted – a few topics had been sorted out beforehand, so he and the others simply ad-libbed.

Left: Elvis chatting to Colonel Tom Parker during a break in filming on *Change of Habit*. Elvis played a doctor working in a big city slum, with Mary Tyler Moore as one of three young nuns assigned to do social work in his clinic. Since she is in plain clothes Elvis does not realize she is a nun and falls in love with her, and she must decide between him and the Church. The movie did not reveal which path she took, leaving the audience to decide for themselves.

Standing ovation for live performance

At a press conference following the opening night of the first of the Las Vegas shows in summer 1969. Newsmen from all over the world had gathered to see him perform and Elvis told them 'I'm really glad to be back in front of a live audience. I don't think I have ever been more excited than I was tonight.' The show had been the first time he had performed in public for more than eight years, and he had received four standing ovations.

'Suspicious Minds' was released the following September – it went on to become a top ten single and one of Elvis's signature tunes. In 1969, Elvis also had several other top ten hits – including 'Don't Cry Daddy' and 'In the Ghetto'.

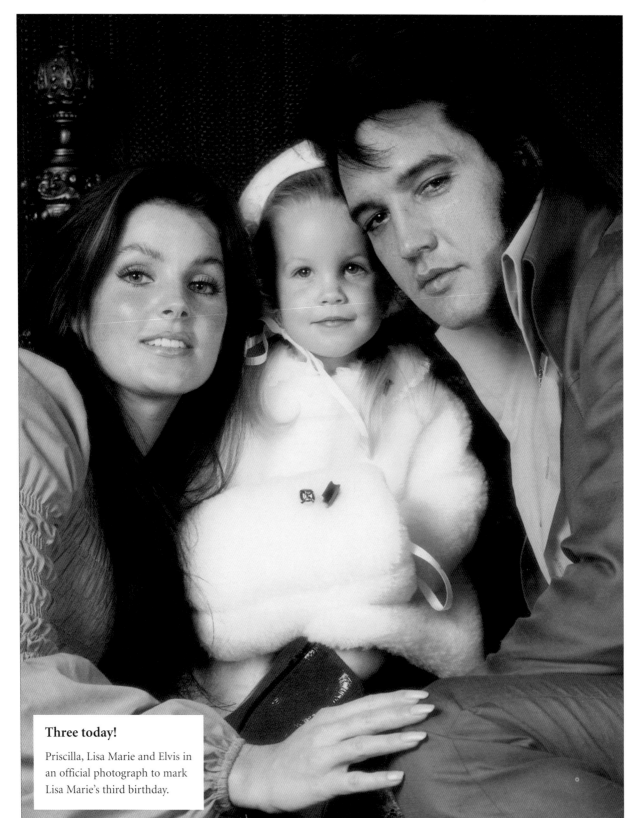

Three today!

Priscilla, Lisa Marie and Elvis in
an official photograph to mark
Lisa Marie's third birthday.

Family time

Despite the appearance of being a happy family,
Priscilla was already becoming dissatisfied with
their marriage. As soon as Elvis began performing
again, he was spending long periods of time away
from home and she and Lisa Marie were left alone.
The pace of the tours meant it was difficult for
wives and families to travel with the group, so
Elvis himself had instigated a strict no-wives rule.

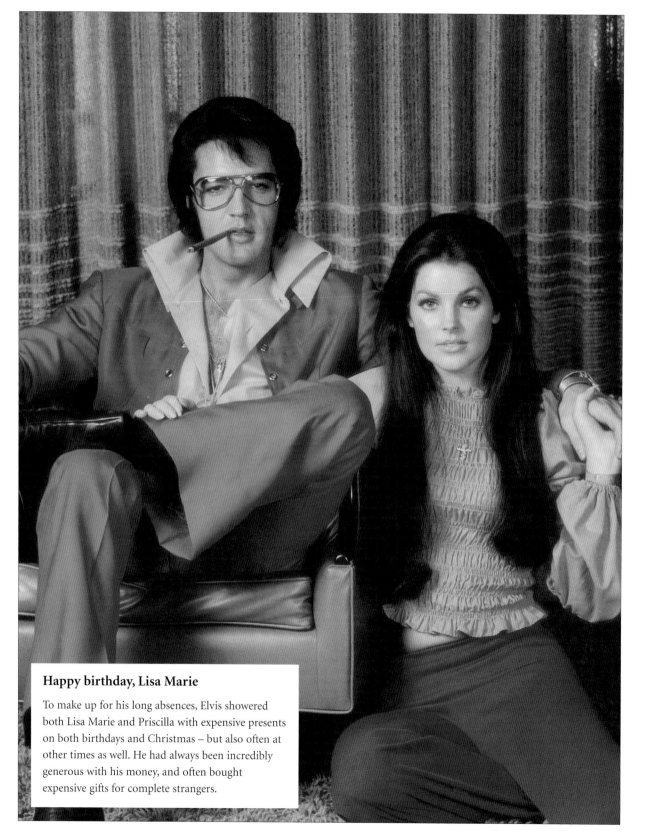

Happy birthday, Lisa Marie

To make up for his long absences, Elvis showered both Lisa Marie and Priscilla with expensive presents on both birthdays and Christmas – but also often at other times as well. He had always been incredibly generous with his money, and often bought expensive gifts for complete strangers.

Chapter Five

Return to Sender

Even at the beginning of the 1970s, it was apparent to most people that Elvis's behaviour was becoming increasingly erratic, not only in private but also onstage. What was not so well known was that this was due to the quantity and mixture of prescription drugs he was taking; they not only caused mood swings, but also increased his paranoia – especially after there were threats to kill or kidnap him during a show. Not long afterwards, he was sworn in as a special deputy so he could carry a hand-gun, and this soon led to an obsession with collecting police badges and firearms. After meeting voice-over artist Paul Frees and learning that he worked as an undercover narcotics agent – complete with an official Bureau of Narcotics and Dangerous Drugs badge – Elvis was determined to get a BNDD badge for himself. Having failed to get one from the Bureau, Elvis simply asked President Nixon for one instead, not only getting in to see the then US President at the White House, but also securing the sought-after badge.

It had now become evident that Elvis and Priscilla were drifting apart – although the reason for her continued absence from his side was at first explained away as due to the work she had been overseeing on a new house being built in Monovale. Elvis carried on much as he had always done; there were women virtually on tap when he needed the company, and often it was indeed just that – for company. Many women said later that when they spent the night with him, nothing happened except perhaps a little kissing – he just didn't want to sleep alone. However, there were also several more prolonged affairs – Elvis had always found it impossible to be faithful to one woman for long. The drugs he was taking often made him difficult to deal with and most women soon tired of a role that was always on his terms, and often seemed to be that of mother rather than lover.

By the end of 1971, Priscilla had developed an interest in karate … and in martial arts expert Mike Stone. After taking Lisa Marie to spend Christmas at Graceland, she told Elvis that she no longer loved him, and returned to Hollywood before the New Year. Two months later she told him about Mike Stone. Elvis was furious that she preferred another man to him, even though he had never been faithful to her, and soon began to date former beauty queen Linda Thompson, who moved into Graceland later that year.

After the success of his recent Las Vegas show, Elvis had embarked on a tour of America, breaking box office records wherever he went; he also appeared regularly for long 'residency' bookings in Las Vegas and at nearby Lake Tahoe. From 1969 to 1977 he played a total of almost 1,100 concerts despite his failing health towards the end of that time. Although, at the start, he obviously enjoyed being back on the stage, towards the end he was really just going through the motions and even the most ardent fans were often disappointed. Many people wondered why he continued with such a punishing schedule, but it was principally for the money.

Elvis had established a costly lifestyle, with large numbers of hangers-on as well as family members relying on him for a living. He was also outrageously generous – not only to people he knew well but also to perfect strangers. He often gave away cars, expensive jewellery and money, and even bought houses for several of his associates. And it was not only Elvis's own lifestyle that had to be maintained. The Colonel had once had a reputation for never spending his own money; he and his wife lived at the William Morris Agency's expense in a house in Palm Springs and he made sure that everyone contributed to the expense of his staff and office space. However, once Elvis had started to appear regularly at Las Vegas, the Colonel developed a passion for gambling

The success of the *Comeback Special* convinced Elvis to go back to touring. At the Houston Astrodome in February 1970, he shows off a new, tousled hairstyle.

Opposite: Although Elvis told people that he would like to do more relaxed and laid-back shows, he knew the audience expected him to throw all his energy into a performance so he continued to give them what they wanted.

and regularly lost at least $1 million a year at the roulette wheel. Many of his close associates became concerned, but found themselves unable to do anything to stop what was happening. The Colonel just told everyone to leave him alone, that it was no business of theirs how he spent his own money, but it was obvious that his gambling had become an obsession that was out of control. Ironically, before they went to Vegas, the Colonel had warned some of the members of the Memphis Mafia not to get hooked on gambling and now he had fallen into the trap himself.

Despite his problems, the Colonel was not one to neglect business and he soon had another mega-deal organized. *Elvis: Aloha From Hawaii,* was a concert on a grand scale that would be broadcast around the world by satellite. Even Elvis was caught up in the excitement of the event, losing some weight for the show and picking out songs that he had not recorded before. Linda Thompson seemed good for him: her sunny personality lifted his mood and she was happy to be with him constantly, attending to his every need. It almost seemed as if Elvis might have turned a corner, as if from now on things would improve.

Unfortunately, this was just an illusion. The Colonel could not understand why Elvis was becoming so irresponsible, and they were soon no longer communicating effectively. Things came to a head in Las Vegas when Elvis made derogatory comments onstage about the management of the Hilton hotel, which now owned the former International. The Colonel was livid and they had a furious argument, with Elvis firing the Colonel just as he quit. They did not speak to each other for several weeks afterwards.

The cocktail of drugs he was taking also made Elvis so ill that he missed several shows, and later in the year at Lake Tahoe, the same thing happened again. In an attempt to stop what was happening, a private detective was hired to find out the source of Elvis's drug supplies. Three doctors and a dentist were identified, but little further action was taken.

Those around him seemed to believe that Elvis would pull through on his own, just as he had dropped other things when they ceased to interest him.

In October 1973, Elvis's divorce from Priscilla was finalized. A few days later he was admitted to the hospital, and the papers reported he had collapsed because he was so upset about the end of his marriage. The reality was that he had suffered a serious reaction to the drugs he was taking. His doctor, George Nichopoulos, brought in a team of specialists who stabilized his condition, and then began an investigation into just what had caused the problem. Finally they discovered that Elvis was getting almost daily doses of pethidine, a painkiller, and was seriously addicted. He was also regularly taking tranquilizers, cortisone and sleeping pills, as well as adopting various quick-fix diets whenever he needed to lose weight in a hurry. All this had done him considerable physical damage. After quietly undergoing a drug withdrawl program in the hospital, Elvis was nursed back to health. His room at Graceland was searched and all drugs removed before he returned home, where he spent the next couple of months recuperating. His collapse had scared him so much that, for a while at least, he was a good patient, and Dr Nichopoulos visited him almost daily to try and moderate his diet and to supervize his medication.

When he returned to Las Vegas towards the end of January 1974, Elvis was thinner and in better shape than he had been for some years. A few weeks after the end of that Vegas season, he began touring again, and this time Dr Nichopoulos came with him. Elvis was still taking an assortment of painkillers, tranquilizers and sleeping pills, but Dr Nichopoulos had worked out a daily program to keep things on an even keel, adding multivitamins and substituting placebos for some of the drugs when he thought Elvis didn't really need them. Although, on the surface, things had stabilized, onstage Elvis was still behaving

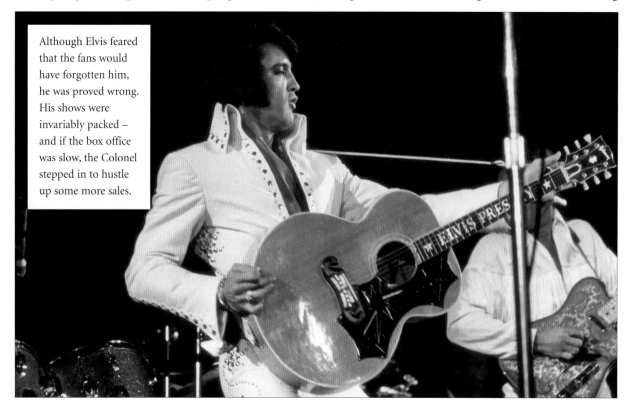

Although Elvis feared that the fans would have forgotten him, he was proved wrong. His shows were invariably packed – and if the box office was slow, the Colonel stepped in to hustle up some more sales.

in an eccentric way. The music had become rather mundane, he no longer sang with any discernible emotion, and he often stopped singing and addressed the audience on any subject that happened to take his fancy, including his personal life, karate and religion.

Meanwhile, sales of his new record releases were down. His last few recording sessions had generated little suitable material – perhaps due to his health problems, or maybe just because of tiredness after years of almost continuous performing. Since RCA had purchased all rights to Elvis's back catalogue from the Colonel for $5.4 million in 1973, it now began to concentrate on releasing a series of records containing his old material; sales of these far outstripped those of Elvis's current releases and were not subject to royalties.

Elvis's commitment to his new health regime did not last long. By the end of 1974 he had put on weight again and was severely depressed. He spent his 40th birthday in seclusion, and at the end of January, was rushed back into the hospital and treated again to get his use of drugs back under control. While he was there, his father Vernon had a heart attack and joined him in the same hospital. After leaving hospital, Elvis stayed at Graceland to rest and lose more weight. Again, his resolution did not last long, and within a few months, he was gaining weight and finding the drugs he wanted, despite all attempts to stop him. During concerts he often appeared exhausted, but the fans still loved him. In August, several shows in Las Vegas had to be cancelled due to Elvis's ill health, and he was re-admitted to hospital. By now, Linda Thompson had realized that she would never be able to save Elvis from himself, and with great reluctance she began to make a life away from him.

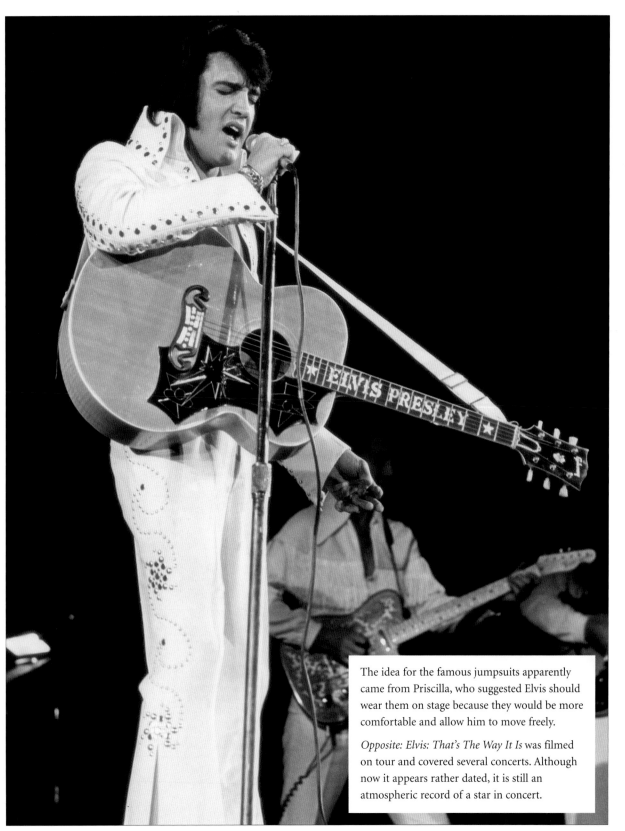

The idea for the famous jumpsuits apparently came from Priscilla, who suggested Elvis should wear them on stage because they would be more comfortable and allow him to move freely.

Opposite: Elvis: That's The Way It Is was filmed on tour and covered several concerts. Although now it appears rather dated, it is still an atmospheric record of a star in concert.

With cancelled engagements, a restricted touring schedule and no new record releases, there wasn't much money coming in. Vernon persuaded Elvis that they needed to cut expenses and three members of the Memphis Mafia were fired – Red and Sonny West, and Dave Hebler. Soon afterwards, the three of them got together with journalist Steve Dunleavy to write a book exposing what life had been like with Elvis. He was deeply upset at what he saw as a betrayal, and also worried about what his fans would think of some of the more lurid revelations.

With his entourage cut back to almost nothing, and Linda Thompson pursuing her own career, Elvis was feeling abandoned and alone. At this point he was introduced to Ginger Alden, a 20-year-old former beauty queen. Although many believed that she never really loved Elvis, he pursued her avidly,

buying her cars and expensive presents, and soon asked her to marry him. She accompanied him on several tours and her presence seemed to give him a new lease of life for a short while.

At the end of July 1977, Lisa Marie came to Graceland for a two-week visit. Elvis seemed in a good mood for most of the time, although he was slightly edgy about his next tour. On August 15, he had a couple of teeth filled and later played some racket-ball, as usual settling down to try to sleep in the early hours of the morning. Despite three doses of medication he was unable to settle, and told Ginger that he would go to the bathroom to read. She woke up early in the afternoon of the 16th to find that she was still alone in bed, and went to investigate. She found Elvis lying on the floor of his bathroom, but she was too late. The King of Rock 'n' Roll was dead.

That's The Way It Is

The premiere of *Elvis: That's The Way It Is* was in November 1970. Elvis is seen playing a guitar during one of the scenes, and he is obviously not as fit, healthy and vibrantly alive as he had appeared in the *Comeback Special* just two years earlier.

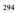

The best man

Elvis was not only best man at the marriage
of his old friend George Klein – he had also
generously paid for the wedding and he
hugged the blushing bride for the benefit
of photographers. It was held in Las Vegas
on 5 December 1970, and Elvis flew a dozen
of his entourage in, also paying for them to
stay at the International in his suite. Klein
was a former DJ and member of the
Memphis Mafia, and had appeared in
small parts in several of Elvis's movies.

Best of friends

Elvis, Priscilla and singer Glen Campbell. Glen Campbell had first worked as a session man for Elvis, but the two of them went on to become close friends.

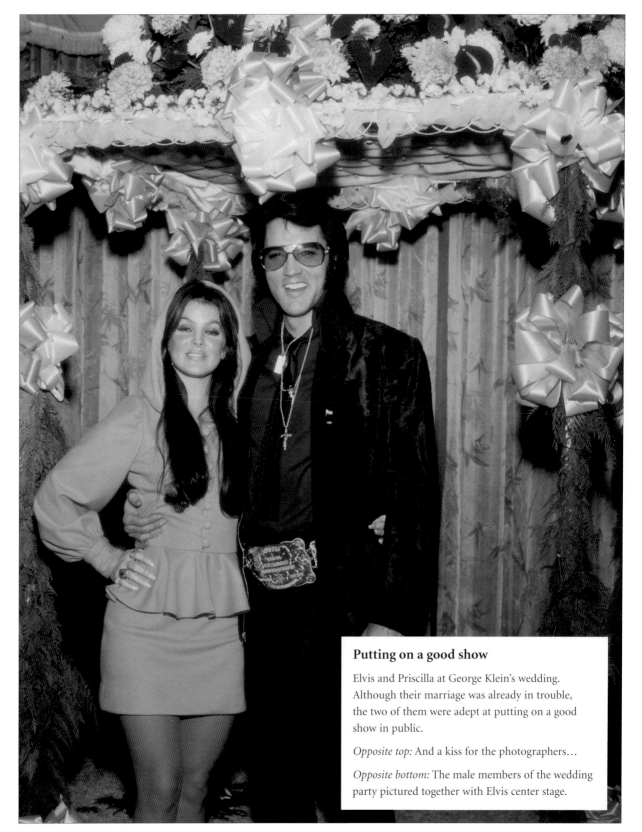

Putting on a good show

Elvis and Priscilla at George Klein's wedding. Although their marriage was already in trouble, the two of them were adept at putting on a good show in public.

Opposite top: And a kiss for the photographers…

Opposite bottom: The male members of the wedding party pictured together with Elvis center stage.

Elvis and Glen

Elvis with Glen Campbell. Although he never smoked cigarettes, Elvis was very fond of cigarillos.

Opposite: One of the bridesmaids also gets a hug. The women very rarely got into the picture – although many of the Mafia were now married, their wives were very much in the background.

Meet the President…

After Elvis wrote to
President Nixon, offering
to help stamp out drugs,
he was invited to the
White House to meet the
President. After Nixon
agreed to give Elvis a
coveted BNDD badge,
Elvis stepped forward
and hugged him – taking
both the President and
his aide off guard.

Below: Sonny West and
Elvis adjust each other's
ties before Sonny's
wedding ceremony, which
was held in Memphis.

Nervous bridegroom Sonny West poses with Elvis. Elvis's 'fur-cloth' black bell-bottom suit had been a Christmas present from Priscilla.

Law enforcers…

Back at Graceland, the men gathered for a group picture, all displaying the deputy's badges that they had recently acquired. Elvis is center stage, flanked by Dr Nichopoulos on the left and Red West on the right, both kneeling. From left to right behind are Billy Smith, former Sheriff Bill Morris, Lamar Fike, Jerry Schilling, Sheriff Roy Nixon, Vernon Presley, Charlie Hodge, Sonny West, George Klein and Mart Lacker.

Right: Elvis proudly displays one of his guns. He had built up quite a collection and even walked down the aisle as best man wearing two guns in a shoulder holster, two pearl-handled pistols in the waistband of his pants and a derringer in his boot.

Elvis, Lisa Marie and Priscilla with Dr George Nichopoulos and his wife. Dr Nick was later accused of over-prescribing drugs to Elvis, but in fact he had fought a losing battle to stabilize an already-established heavy intake.

Star in the desert

When Elvis began appearing in Las Vegas regularly during the 1970s, there was no doubt that he was a major star. The Hilton Hotel chain had taken over the International in June the previous year and before the deal was even signed they were anxious to make sure that Vegas's premier attraction would continue to appear in their hotel.

Elvis on tour

Opposite: A shot from *That's The Way It Is*. Those involved in making the new documentary were deeply involved in their subject. They approached Elvis in concert as if he were a folk hero on a mythic journey. In addition, they had the latest mobile cameras and equipment, which brought movement and spontaneity to the filming.

As well as shots of Elvis performing, the moviemakers – Bob Abel and Pierre Adidge – included backstage material, shots of past glories and candid moments. The final movie is one of the classic records of Elvis's career.

At the beginning, Abel had told Elvis, 'I want to shoot the real you… but you've got to be open with me. If I feel that you're posing or doing something, I'll just turn the camera off.' Elvis appreciated his honesty, and from then on was committed to the project.

Putting on the style in Vegas

The jumpsuits that Elvis wore in Las Vegas have become a symbol that represent this stage of his career. Most of them were designed by tailor Bill Belew, and they became increasingly elaborate. Sometimes they incorporated a cape – either waist or floor-length – and they were decorated with real gemstones and semi-precious jewels.

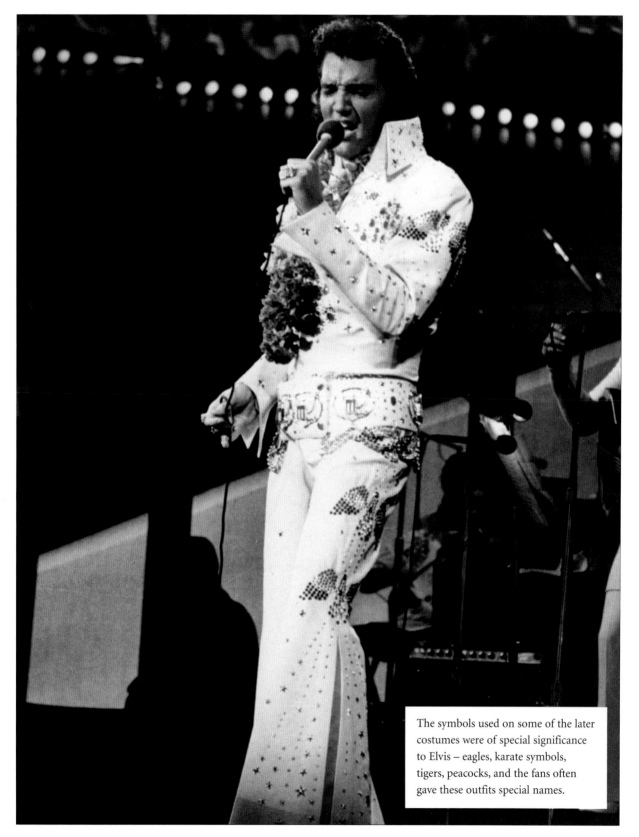

The symbols used on some of the later costumes were of special significance to Elvis – eagles, karate symbols, tigers, peacocks, and the fans often gave these outfits special names.

Spectacular success

The Colonel put together a new project, which was massive in both scale and ambition. *Aloha From Hawaii* was a television special, with Elvis's performance beamed live via satellite to countries all over the world. It was also taped for re-transmission to most of the remaining countries a few days later. Elvis lost weight for the show and looked slim, fit and handsome again. The project was a spectacular success.

The king plays Alabama

Elvis greets Governor George C. Wallace in Montgomery, Alabama, when he performed there at the Garrett Coliseum. Governor Wallace and his family were among the audience of more than 11,000 who came to see the show.

Elvis increasingly had a problem controlling his weight. His poor diet certainly didn't help, but the additional weight was also due to lack of exercise. He was taking a dangerous combination of prescription drugs and he was hospitalized several times. Many of those close to him tried to cut his drug intake, but Elvis was used to getting his own way. Despite his bloated appearance in some of the shows, the fans still loved him and flocked to all his performances.

Chapter Six

Only Believe

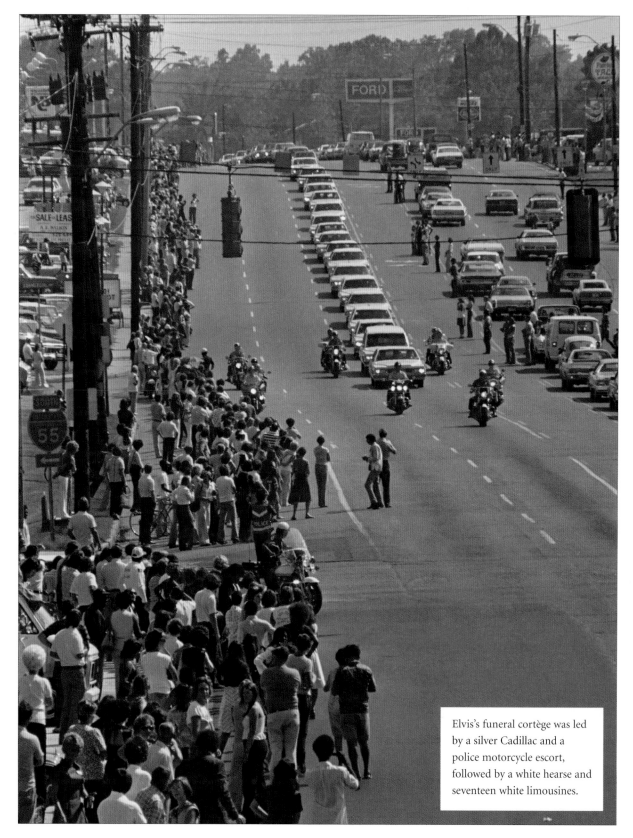

Elvis's funeral cortège was led by a silver Cadillac and a police motorcycle escort, followed by a white hearse and seventeen white limousines.

Right from the start, confusion surrounded the cause of Elvis's death, since the Shelby County Medical Examiner announced to the press that it was due to heart problems (cardiac arrhythmia, or irregular heartbeat) before the autopsy had been completed. In fact, the lab results later confirmed that his death was due to polypharmacy; traces of a total of 14 different medications were found in Elvis's system, with codeine at ten times the recommended level. Elvis had apparently taken the drug after the dental work carried out the day before his death – despite having a mild but long-standing allergy to it. No official announcement was made about the lab results, although rumours of drug abuse quickly began to circulate in the media. In 1979, Dr Nichopoulos was charged with over-prescribing drugs to Elvis and briefly lost his medical licence, but was later found not guilty of any criminal intent.

Elvis's funeral was a private service held at Graceland, with only 200 invited guests, although thousands of fans gathered outside. A cortege of 49 cars followed the white hearse that carried his body to Forest Hill Cemetery, where he was buried next to his mother. The following day an estimated 50,000 fans visited his tomb, and Vernon requested that each should be given a flower from the wreaths and arrangements that were banked up round the cemetery. It had taken 100 vans nearly four hours to move all the floral tributes from Graceland the day before, yet within a few hours they were all gone.

Just 11 days after the burial, three men made what was thought to be a bungled attempt to steal Elvis's body. Charges were dropped after the court was convinced that they had merely been trying to prove that the coffin was empty and that Elvis was still alive. There were fears that it might happen again, so just a couple of months later, both Elvis and his mother were removed from Forest Hill Cemetery and re-interred in the Meditation Garden at Graceland. The Meditation Garden also held a memorial plaque for Elvis's stillborn twin brother, Jesse Garon Presley, and Vernon was buried there after his death in 1979.

The entire Presley estate had been left to Lisa Marie in trust until she was 25, but Priscilla and the other trustees were alarmed to discover how little money was left. The Colonel had wasted no time in arranging a new marketing deal with Vernon, which meant that, for the next few years, he was earning far more from Elvis's name than the estate was. After Vernon's death in 1979, the executors of the Presley estate started an investigation and the courts later ruled that the contract Vernon had signed was void, so the Colonel had to give up all marketing rights.

In 1982 Graceland was opened to the public to raise money to protect Lisa Marie's inheritance, and the Presley estate also began to receive all the income generated through the use of Elvis's name. According to an estimate in *Life* magazine in 1984, the 'Elvis industry' earned ten times more money in the seven years following his death than Elvis had earned in his 23 years of performing. When Lisa Marie turned 25 in 1993, the estate was worth an estimated $100 million and she elected not to take over, but to leave the existing management in place. Elvis Presley Enterprises, Inc is now run as a business, controlling the rights to Elvis's name, and Graceland is a major tourist attraction, one of the most visited historic homes in America.

Elvis is perhaps even more famous today than when he was alive. In the weeks after his funeral, radio stations around the world started to play his music again and several of his records re-entered the charts. Although his music had changed almost out of recognition in the last few years of his life, his death focused attention on the early songs, when he had been a true artist and a major influence on

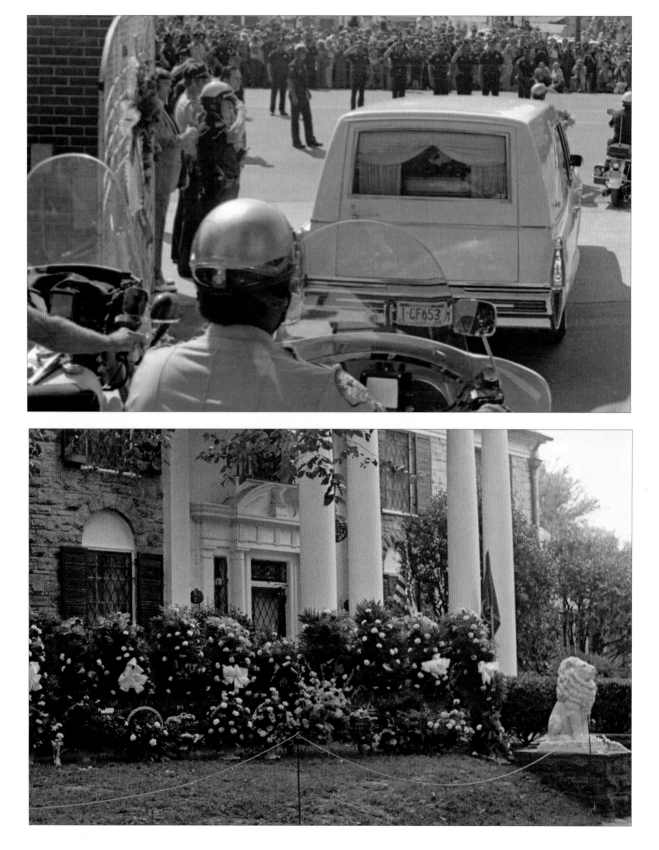

Elvis has left the building…

Elvis's flower-covered casket is carried into the mausoleum at Forest Hill Cemetery. The pall-bearers included Memphis Mafia members Joe Esposito, Charlie Hodge and Lamar Fike, Dr Nichopoulos, and Elvis's cousin Billy Smith.

Opposite top: The hearse with its copper casket leaves Graceland, past saluting policemen. The funeral service had been held in the living room, with a sermon by Reverend Bradley of the Wooddale Church of Christ.

Opposite bottom: Local florists were flooded with over 3,000 orders for flowers and they covered the lawn in front of Graceland. It took four hours to move the flowers to the cemetery before the funeral.

Finally at rest

After an apparent attempt was made to steal Elvis's body just after the funeral, he and his mother were both moved from Forest Hill and reburied in the Meditation Garden at Graceland, in October 1977.

Opposite top: The gray stone mausoleum was surrounded by a bank of flowers and was just a few hundred feet away from Gladys Presley's grave in the same cemetery.

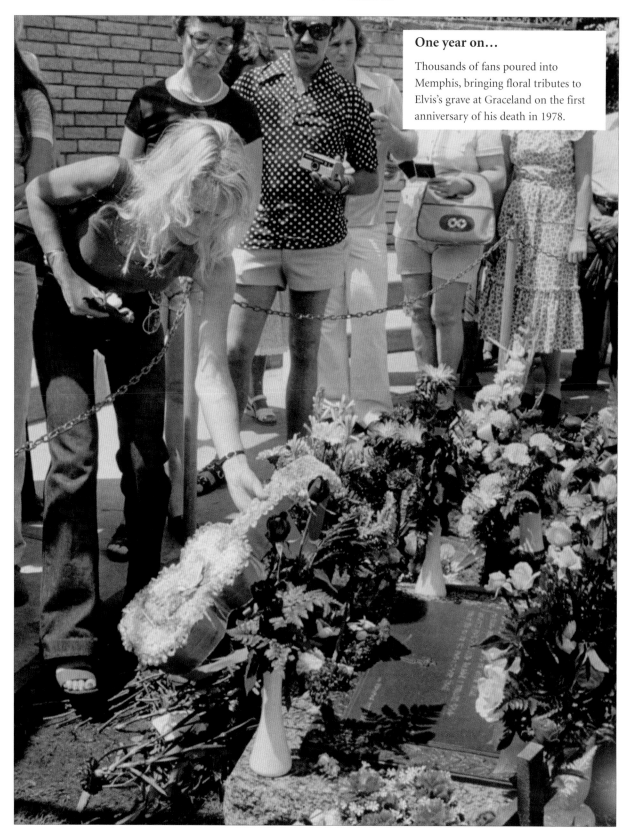

One year on…

Thousands of fans poured into Memphis, bringing floral tributes to Elvis's grave at Graceland on the first anniversary of his death in 1978.

A nine-foot statue of Elvis sculpted
by Eric Parks was erected on Beale
Street in Memphis in 1980 – a fitting
tribute to the city's famous son.

Still a star…

The floral tributes from fans are often extremely elaborate and some are hand-crafted.

Inset: Elvis Presley's star on the Walk of Fame in Hollywood.

The original memorial from Gladys Presley's grave in Forest Hill Cemetery, with the Italian statue specially commissioned by Elvis and Vernon just after her death.

Opposite top: The name and image of Elvis lives on around the world.

Opposite bottom: Elvis's childhood home in Tupelo is now a tourist attraction – although it is furnished with home comforts the Presley's could never have afforded when they lived there.

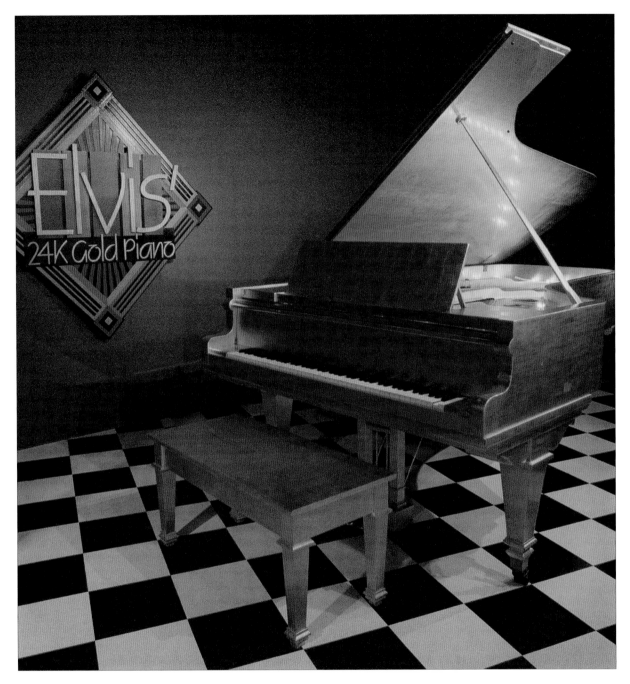

The 1928 Kimball grand piano that Priscilla gave Elvis as an anniversary present, and which she had covered in 24-carat gold leaf both inside and out. It was first placed in the music room at Graceland but is now displayed at Nashville's Country Music Hall of Fame.

Opposite top: Elvis bought this pink Cadillac sedan for Gladys in 1956 – despite the fact she could not drive. It was the only Cadillac that he kept throughout his life and he promised it to Lisa Marie on her 18th birthday.

Opposite bottom: The living room at Graceland has been kept very much as Elvis left it and the décor and furnishings are flamboyant. The stained glass peacock was specially designed for the room – although displaying peacock feathers indoors is supposed to bring bad luck.

Facts and Figures

Elvis Presley has sold an estimated one billion records worldwide – more than anyone else in record industry history.

Certified gold and platinum records in the USA alone, based on current sales standards of half a million for gold and one million for platinum, are as follows:

- 32 gold albums
- 32 platinum albums
- 24 gold singles
- 27 platinum singles
- 6 gold EP singles
- 10 platinum EP singles.

Elvis's chart career looks like this:

- 149 songs in the *Billboard* Hot 100
- 18 songs made No. 1 in the *Billboard* Hot 100
- 9 albums made No. 1 in the *Billboard* Top 100 album chart.

OUND

FROM ELVIS...

He has also received a host of awards and nominations:

- 14 Grammy nominations from the National Academy of Recording Arts and Sciences (NARAS)
- 3 Grammy awards
- 4 recordings in the NARAS Hall of Fame.

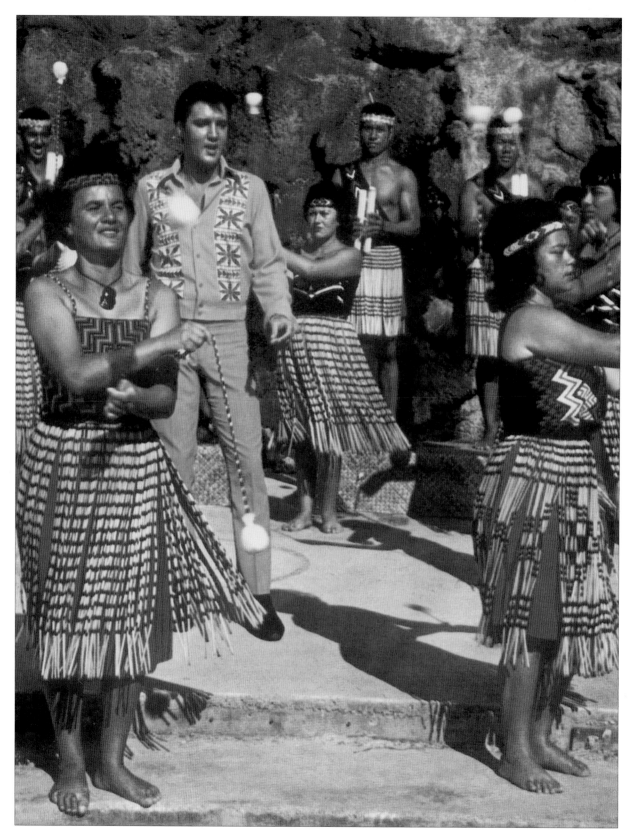